This coloring
belongs to

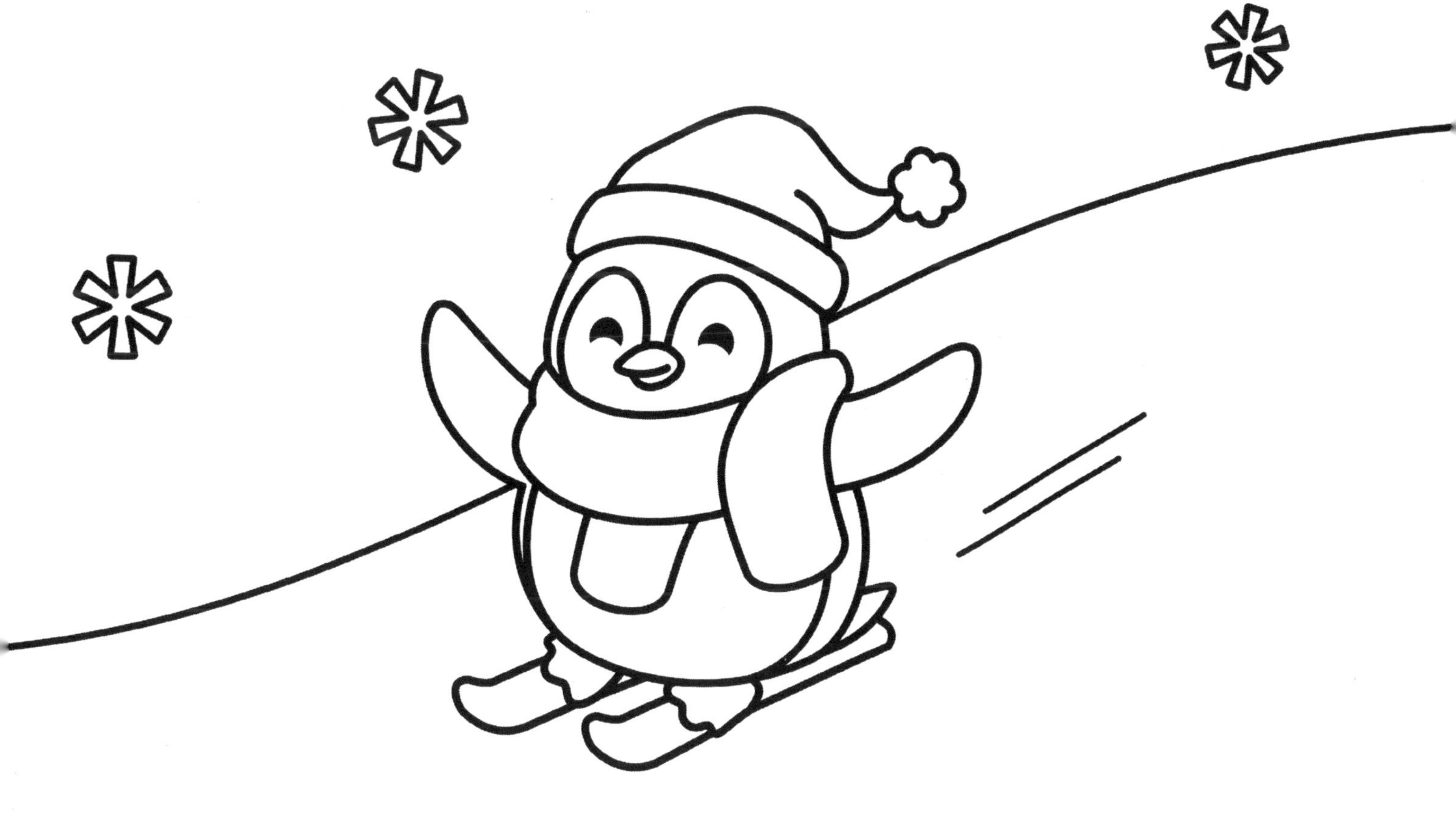

Color test page

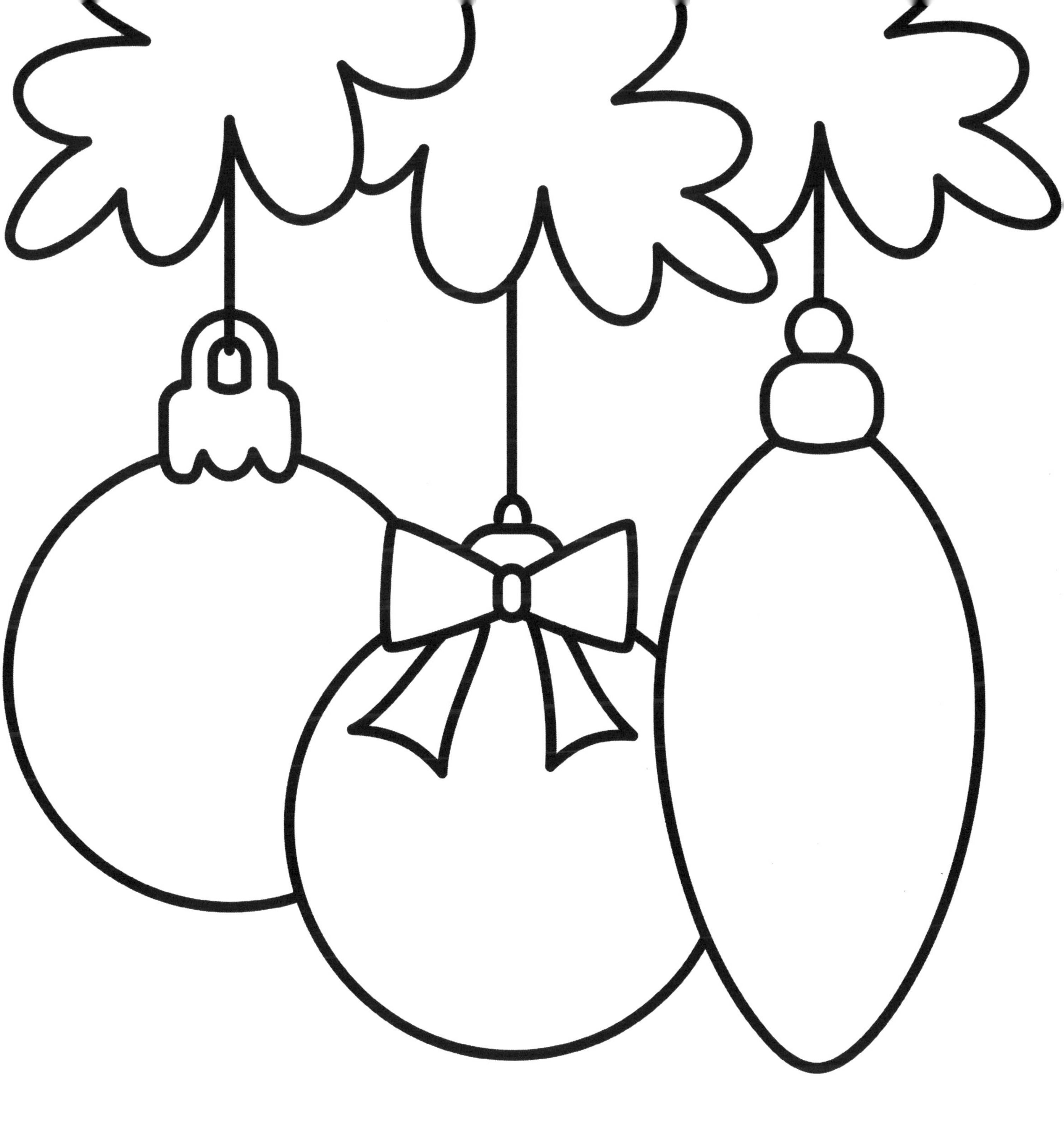

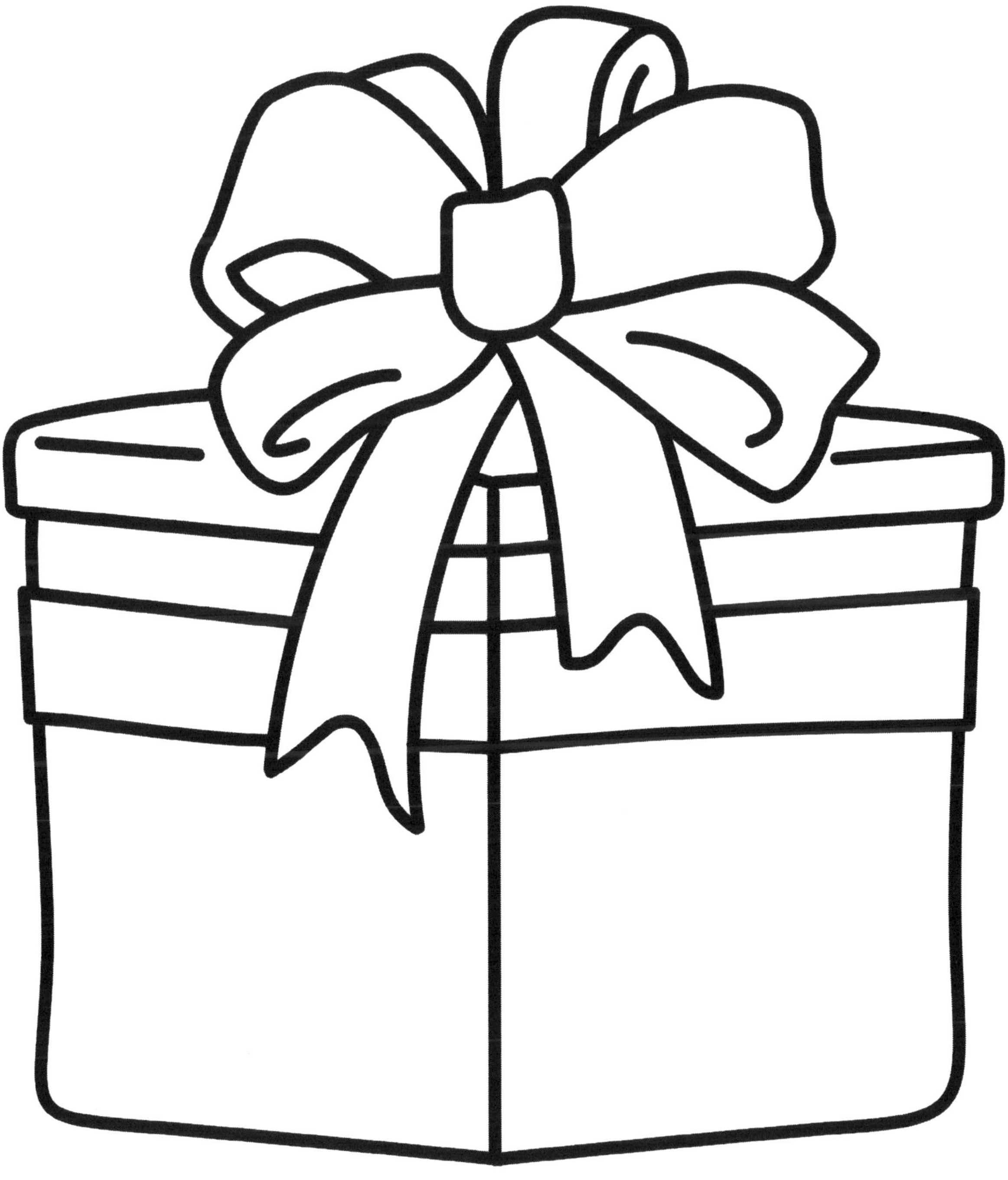

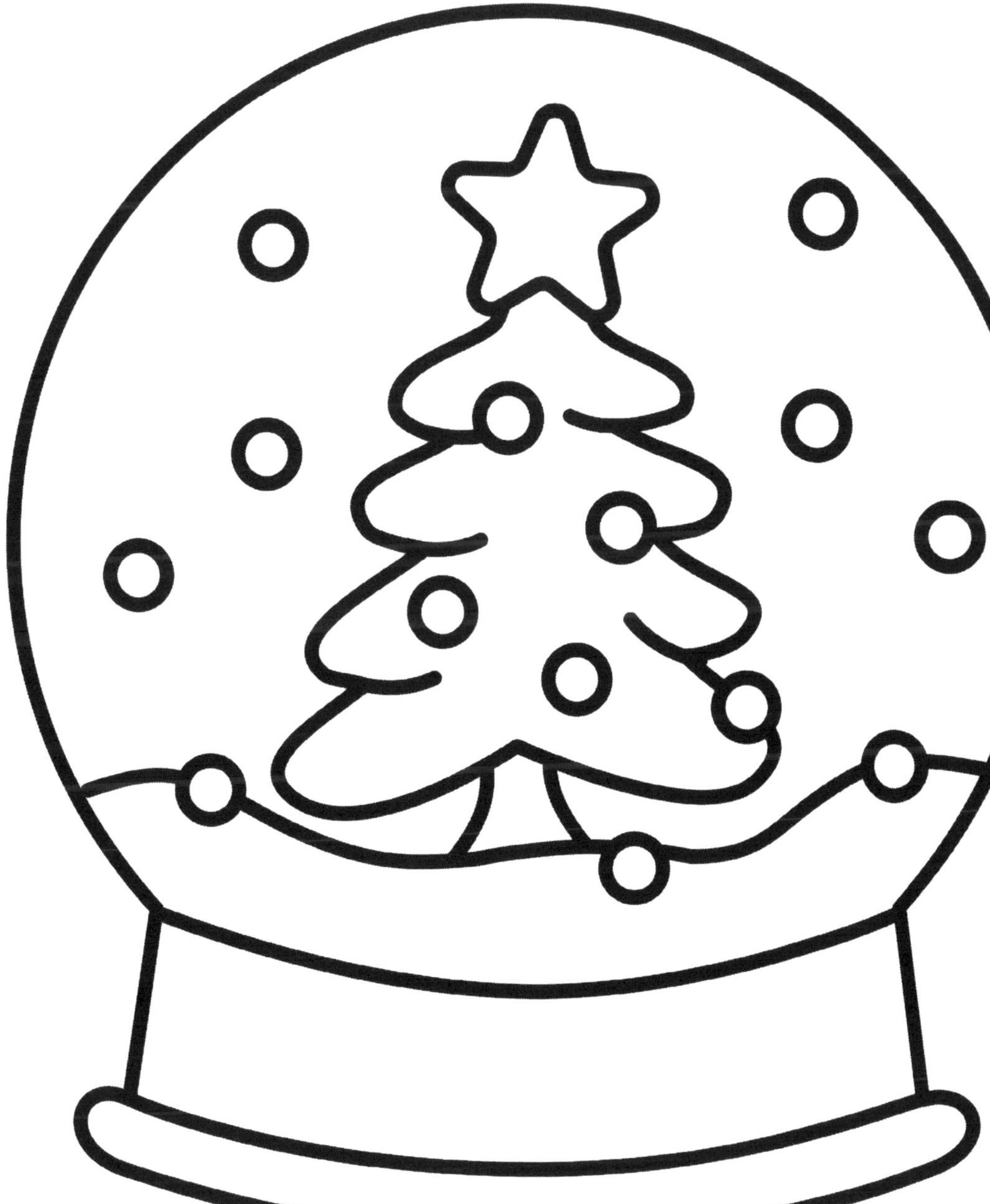

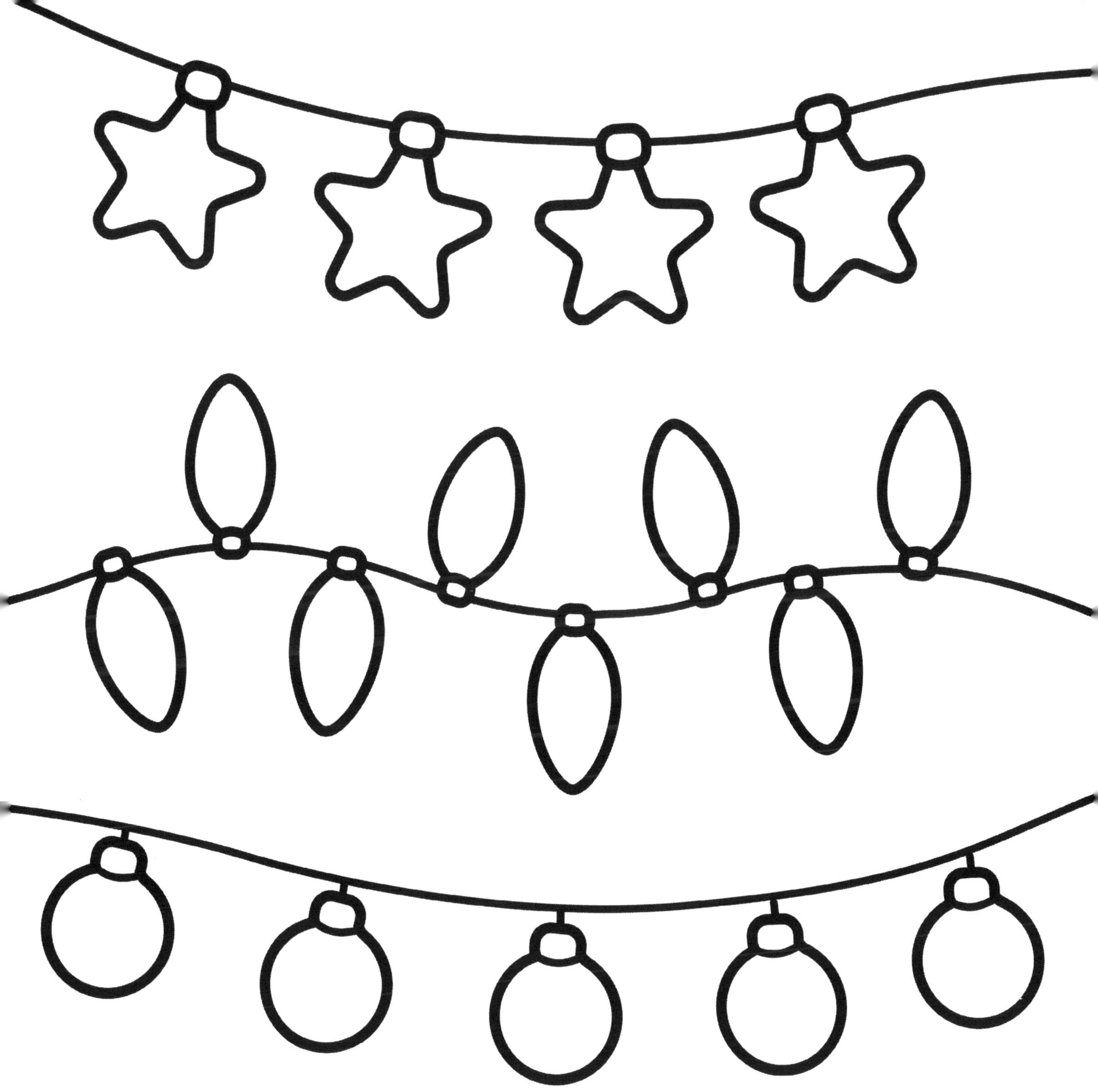

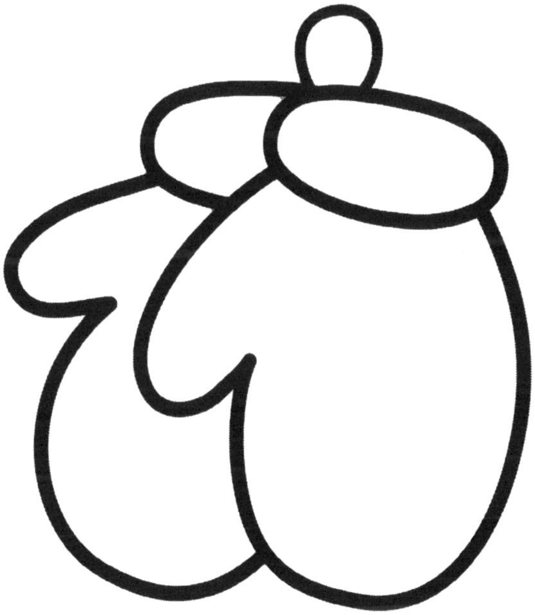
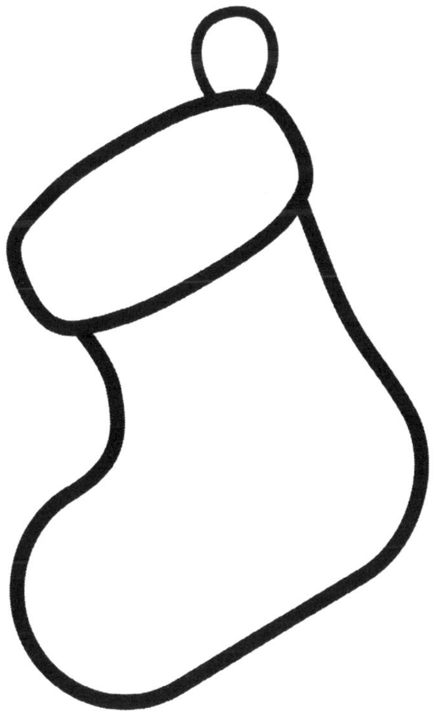
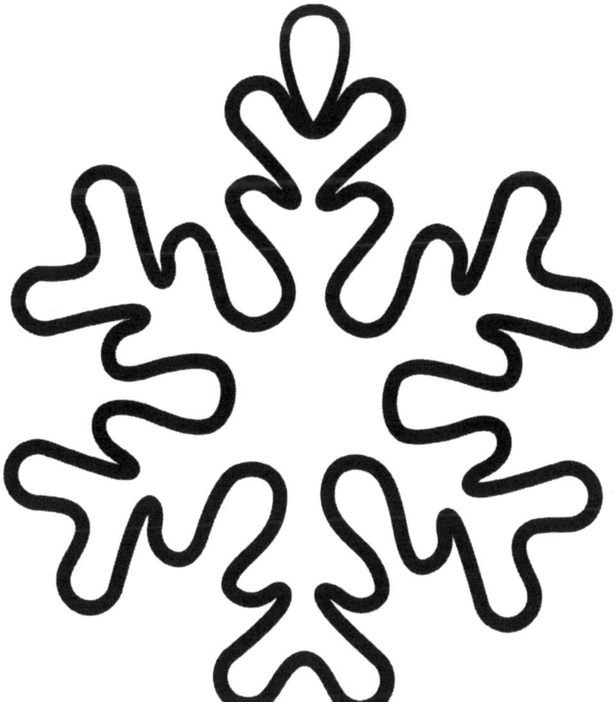

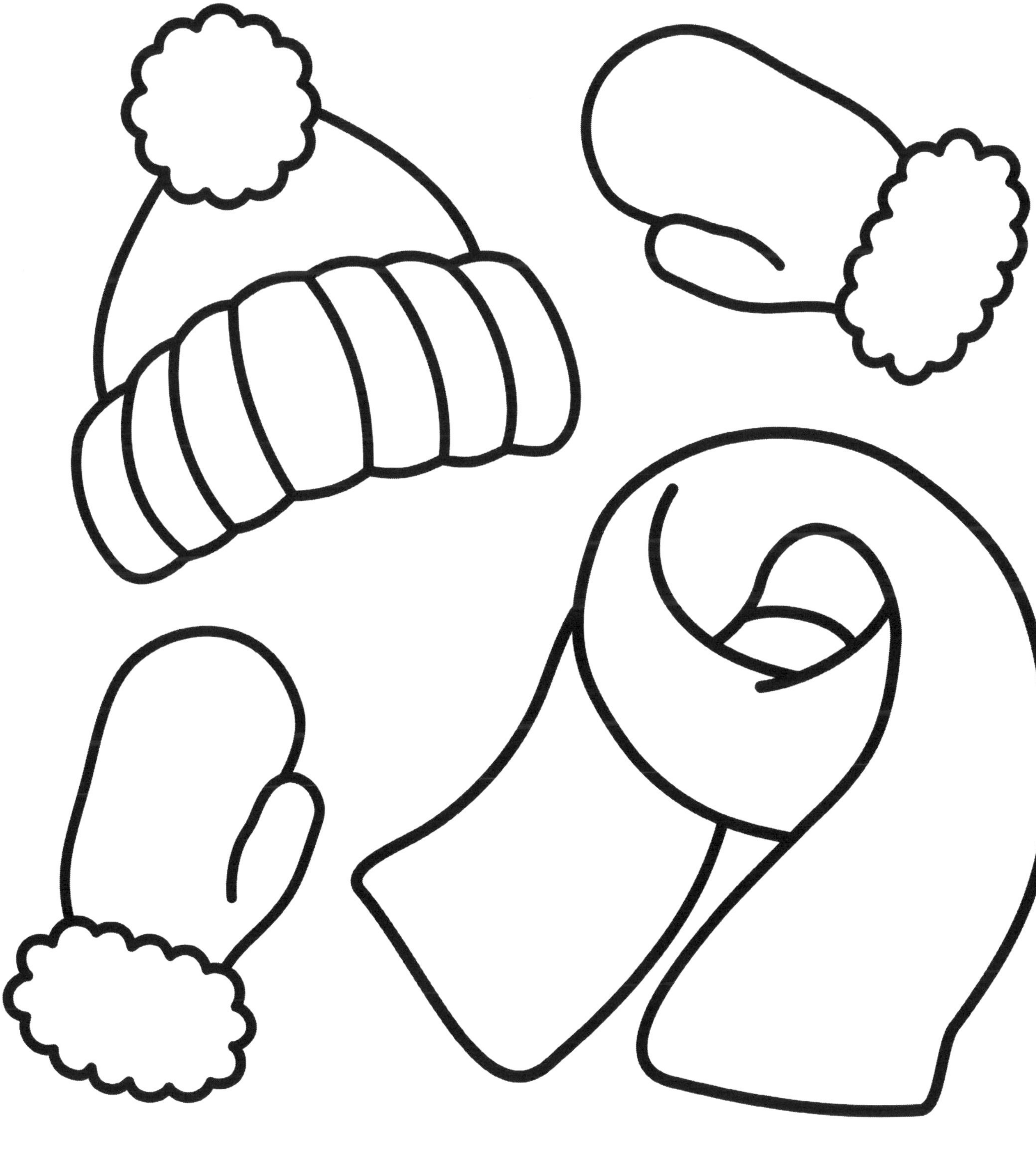

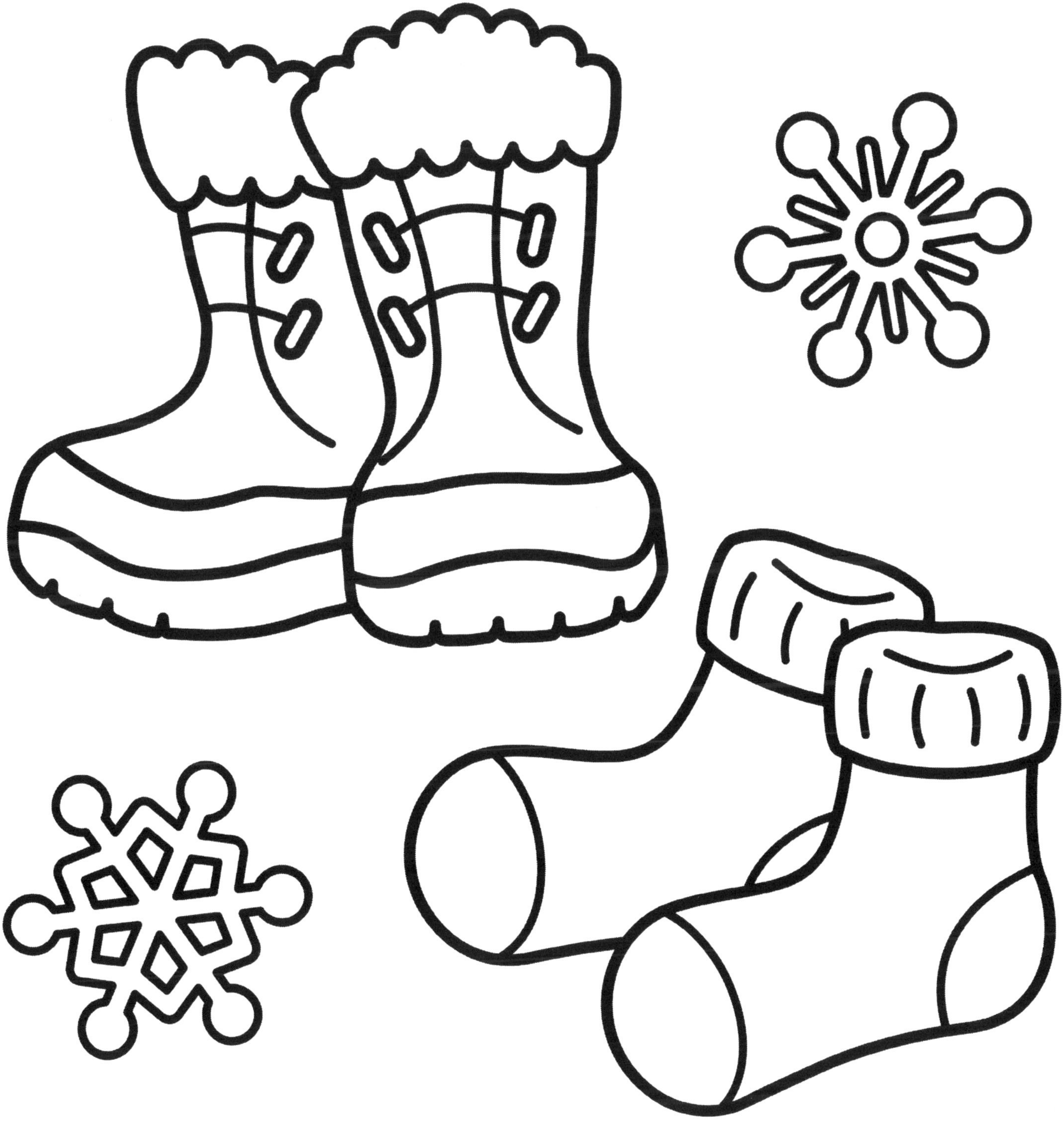

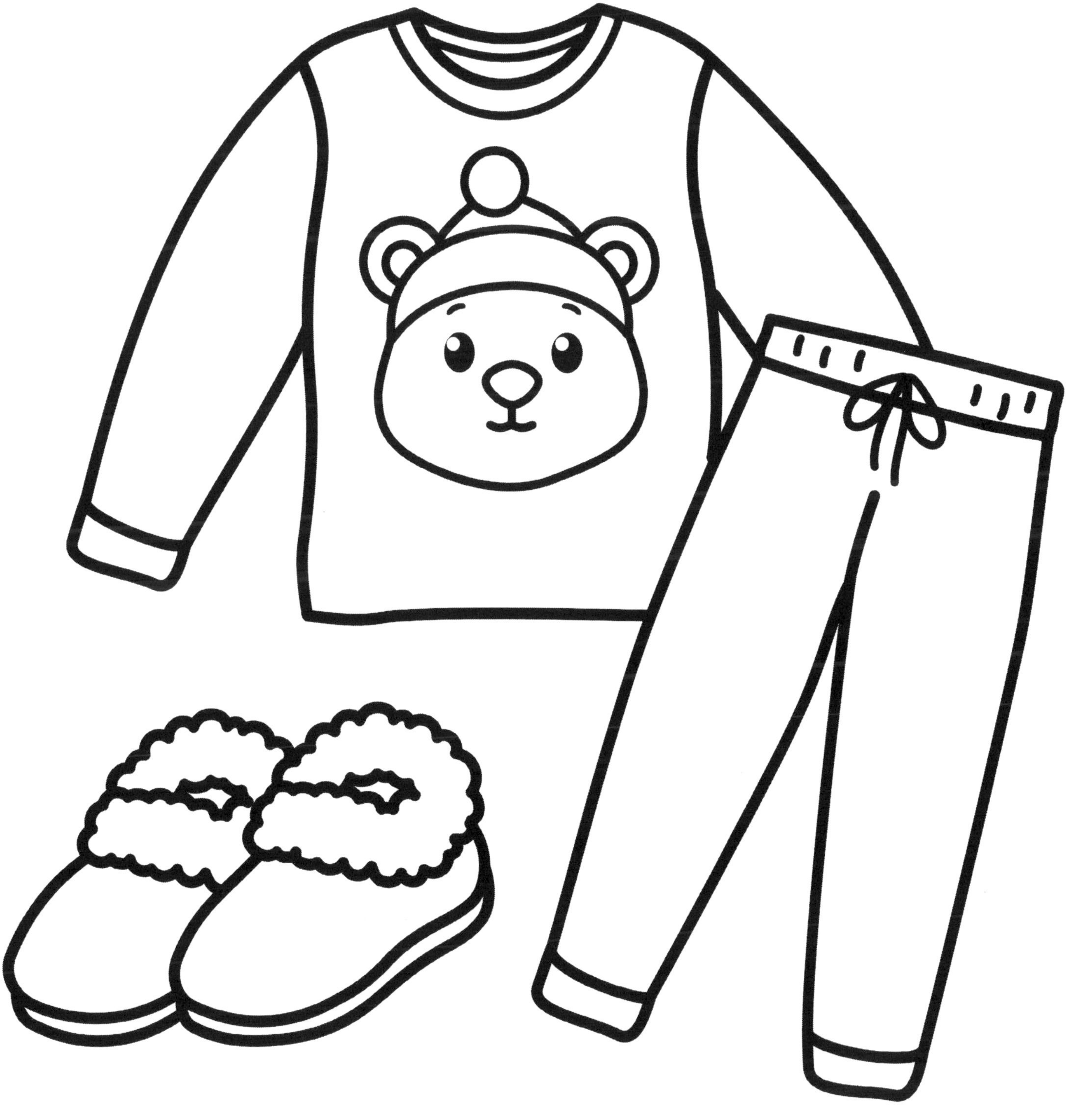

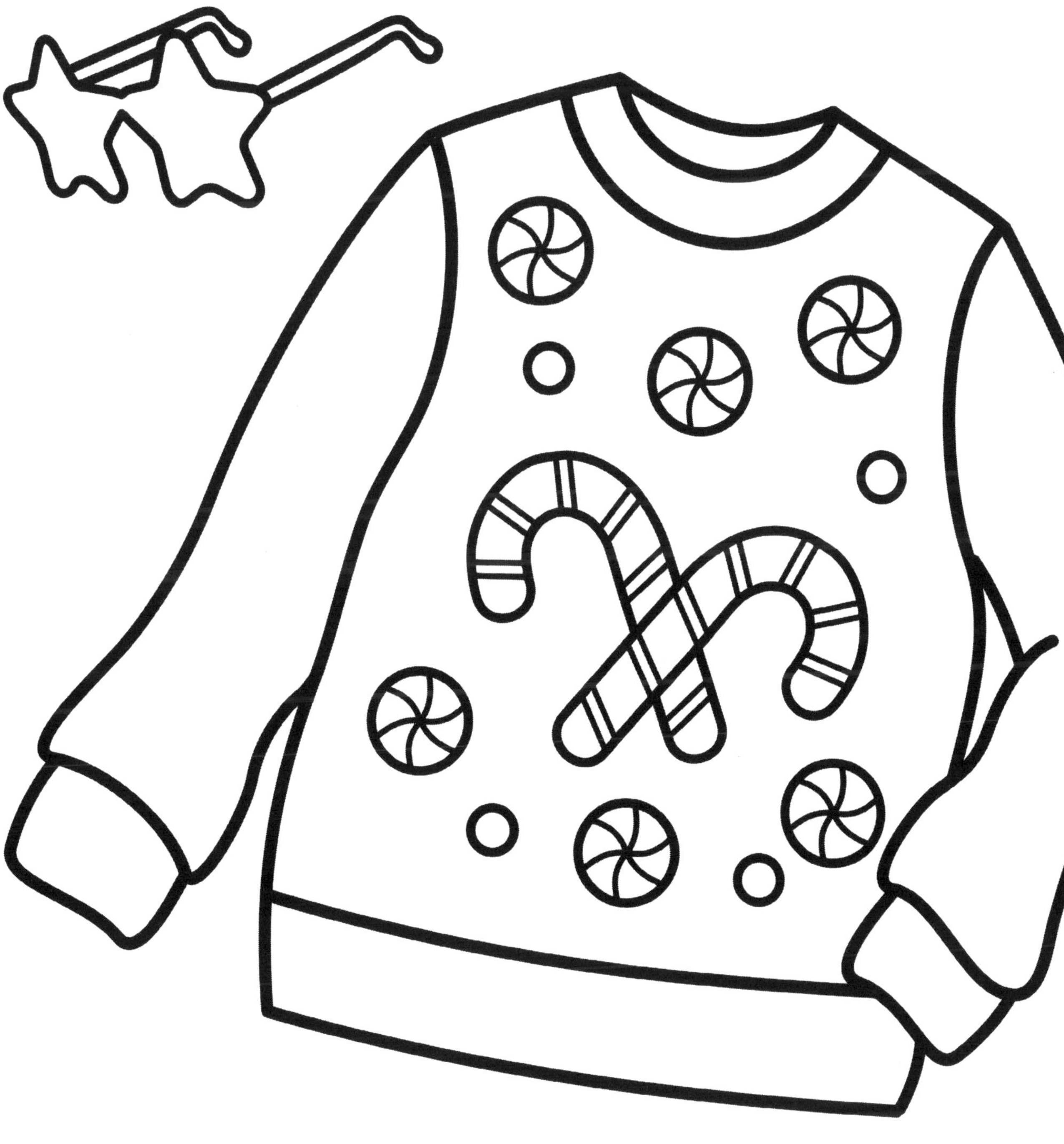

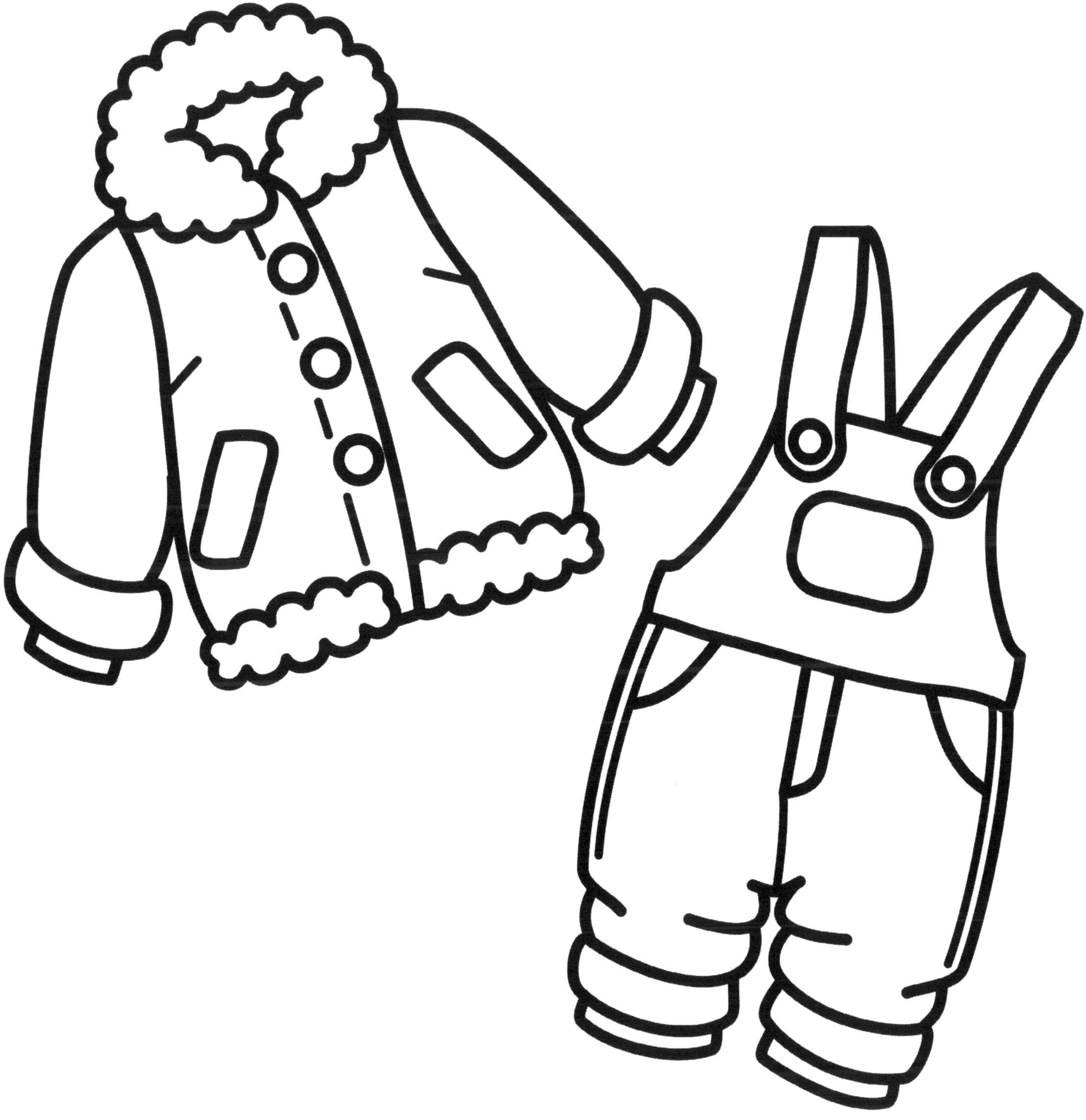

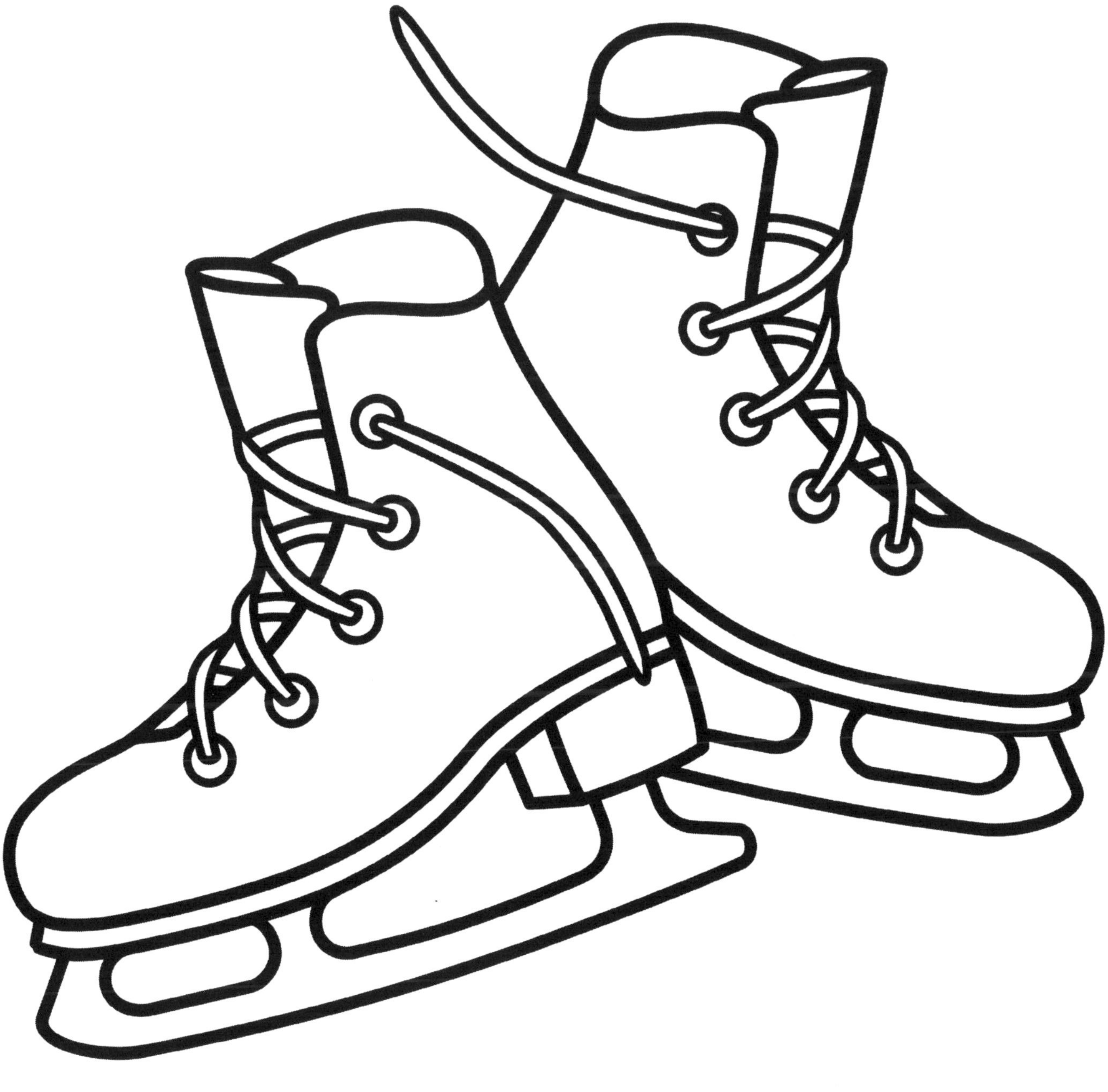

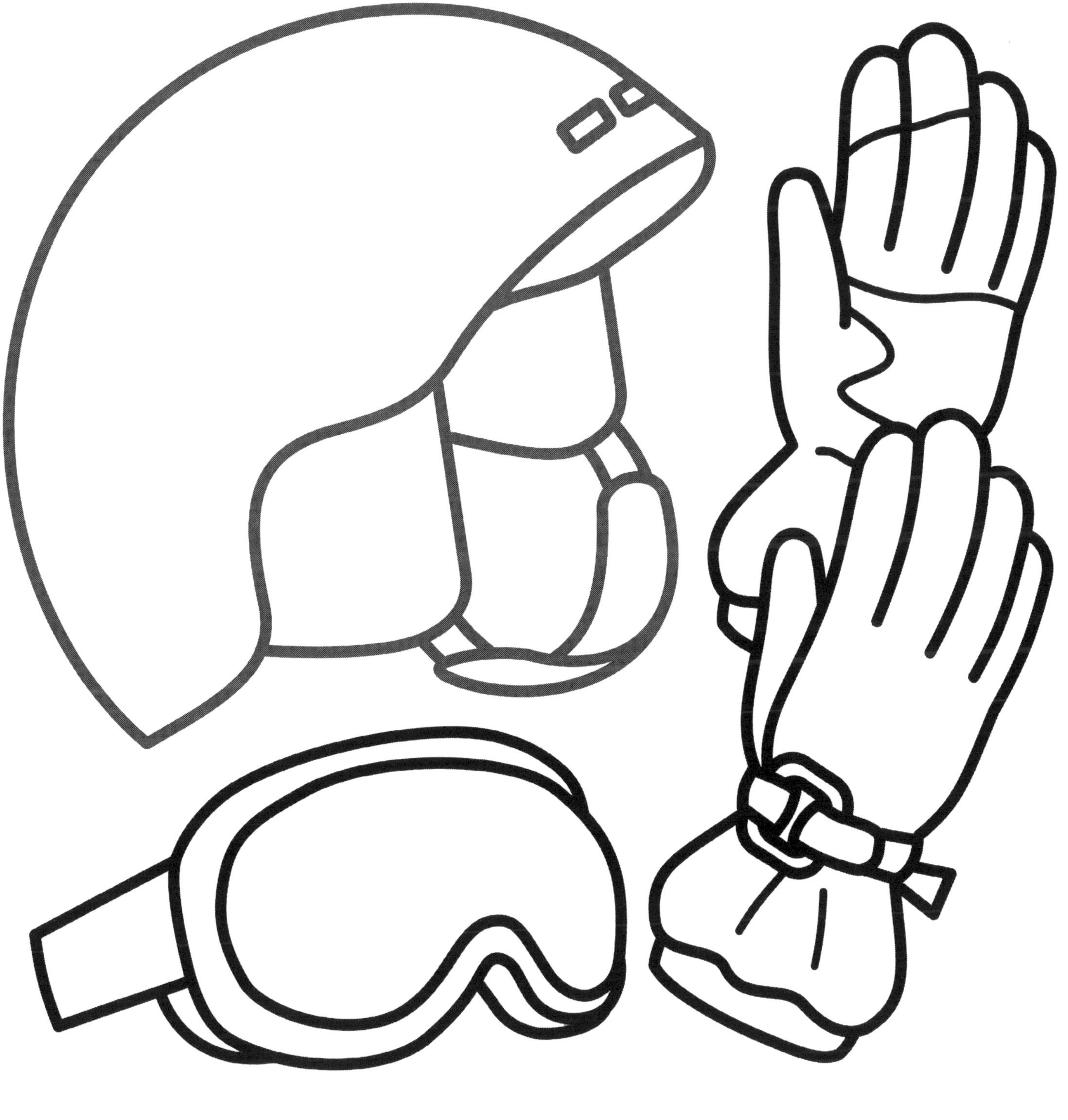

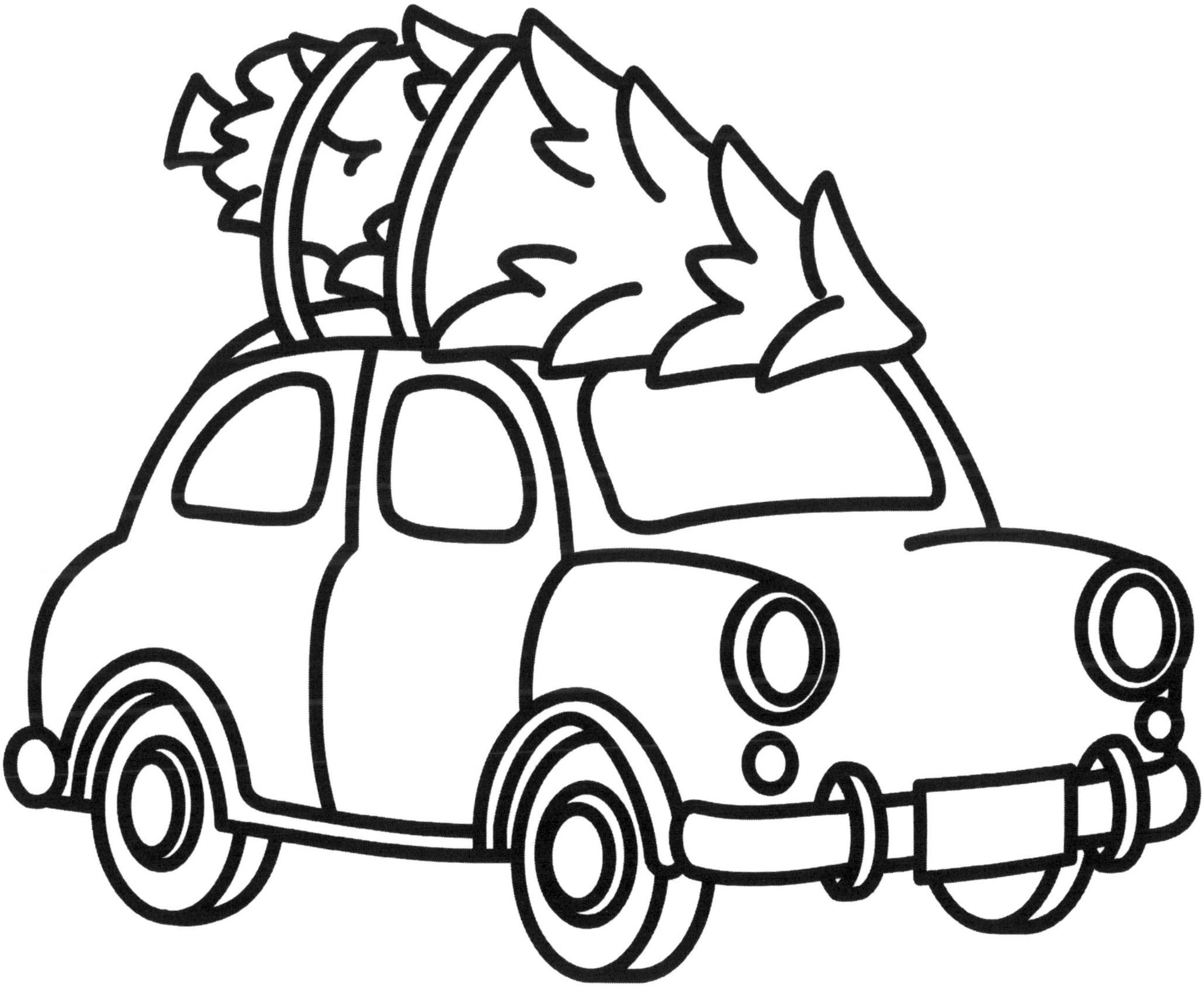

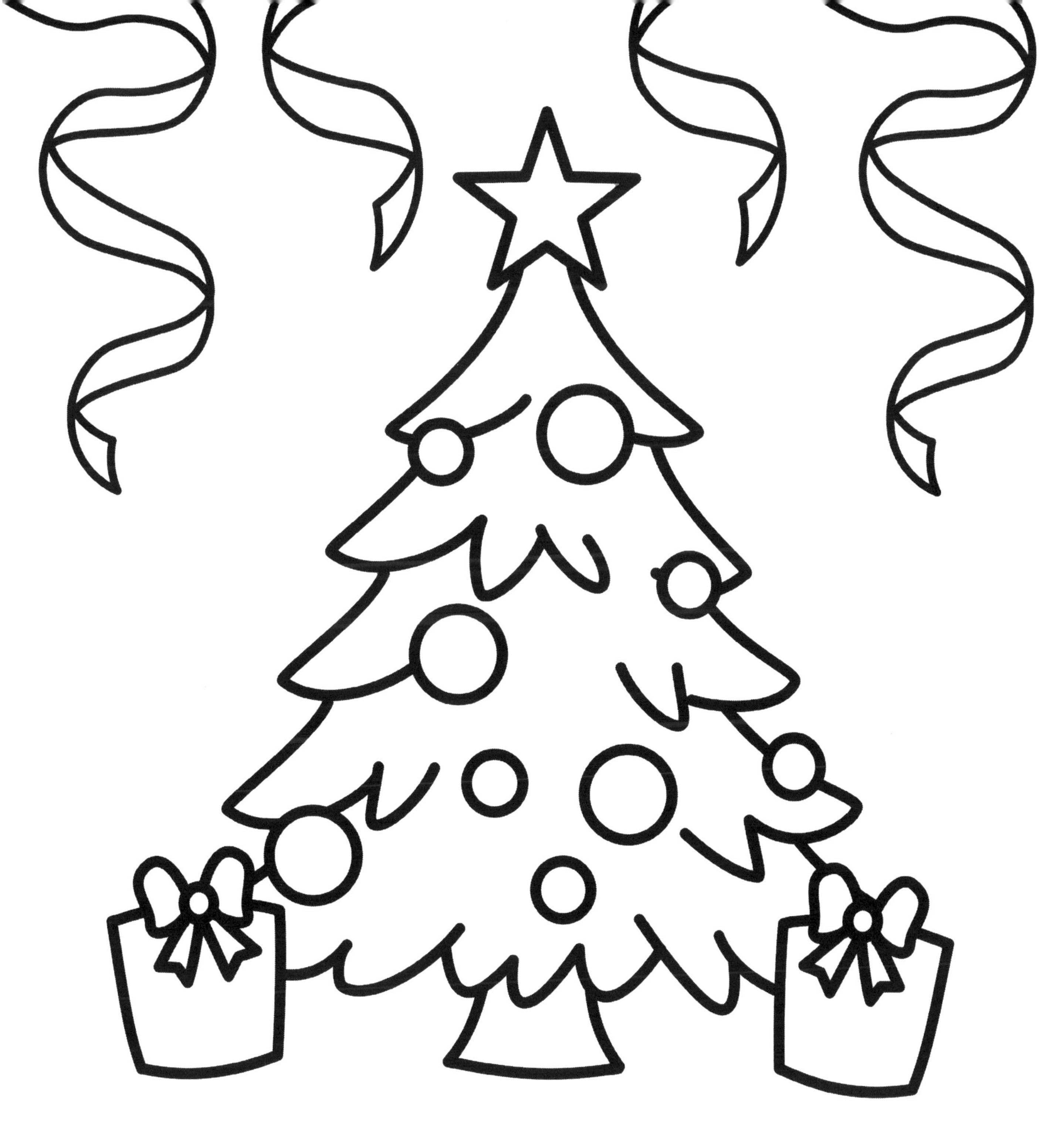

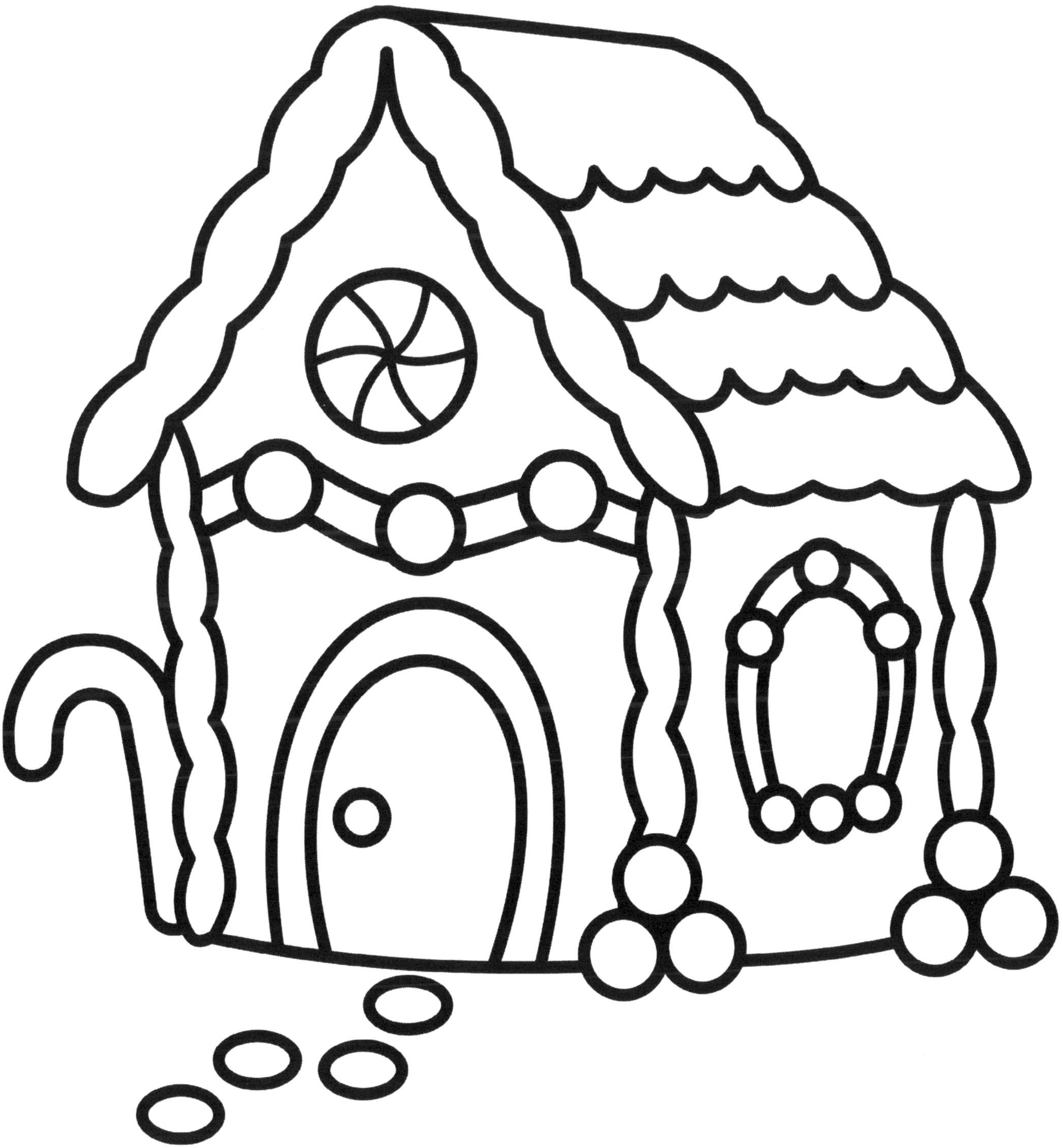

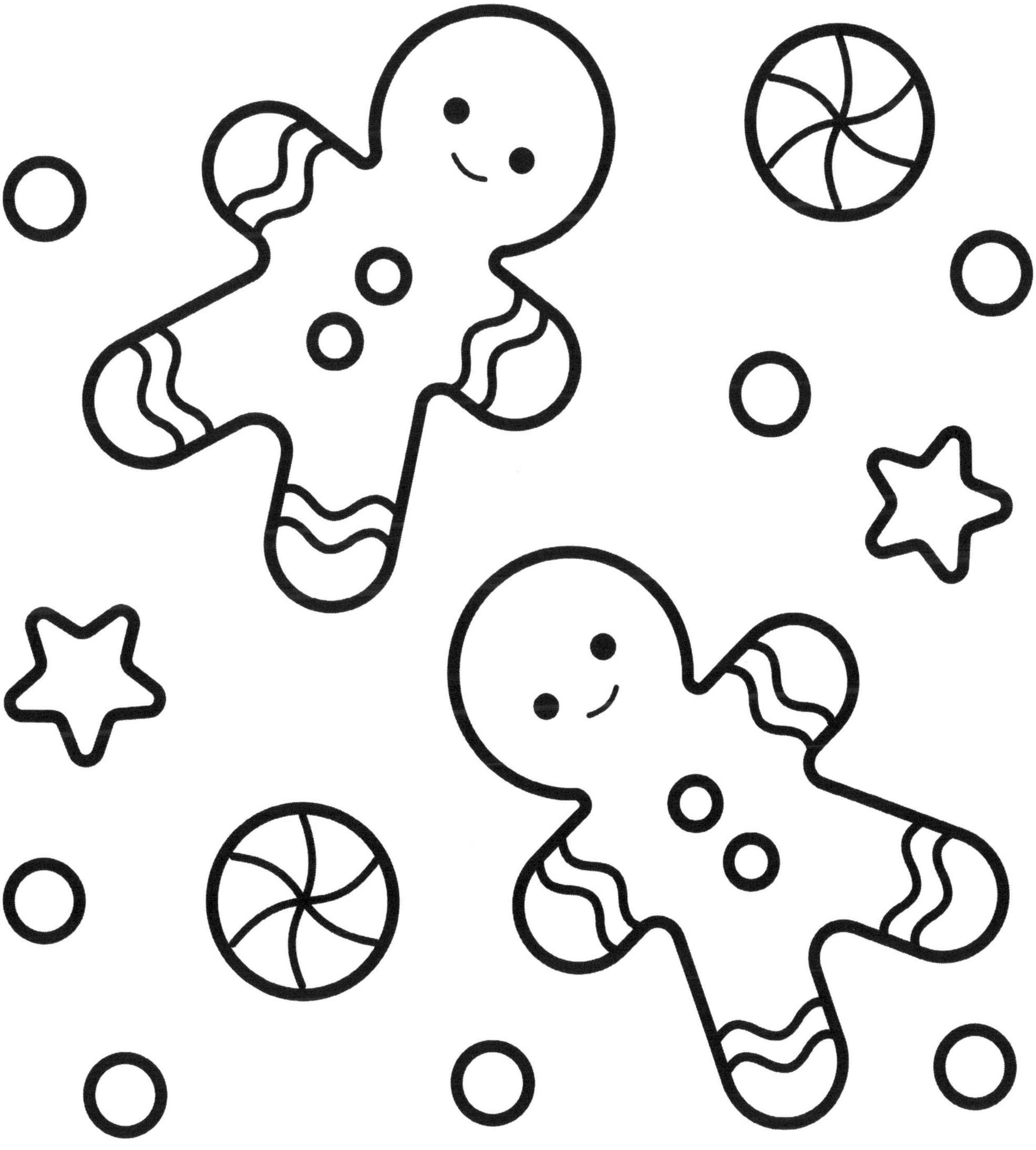

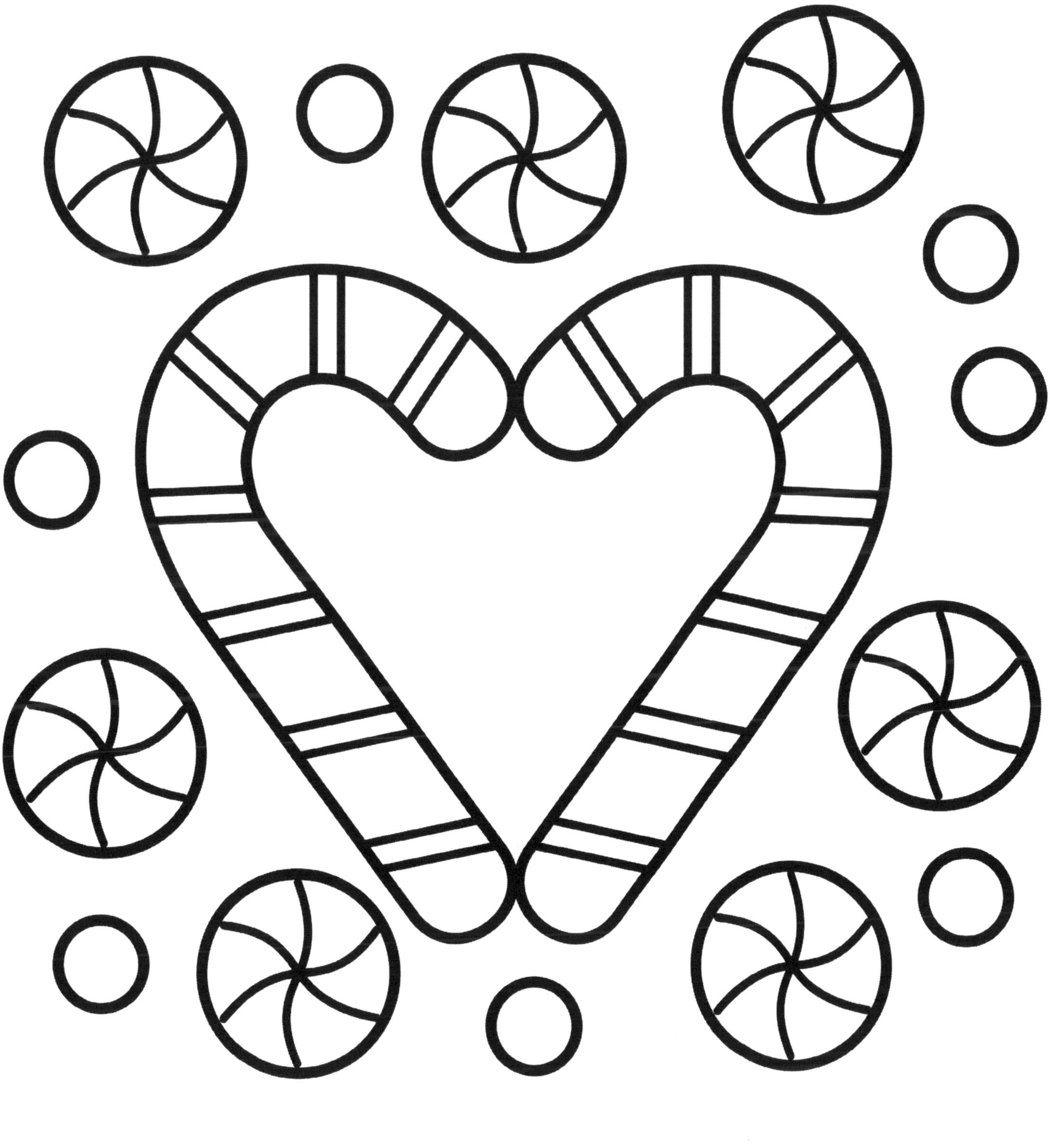

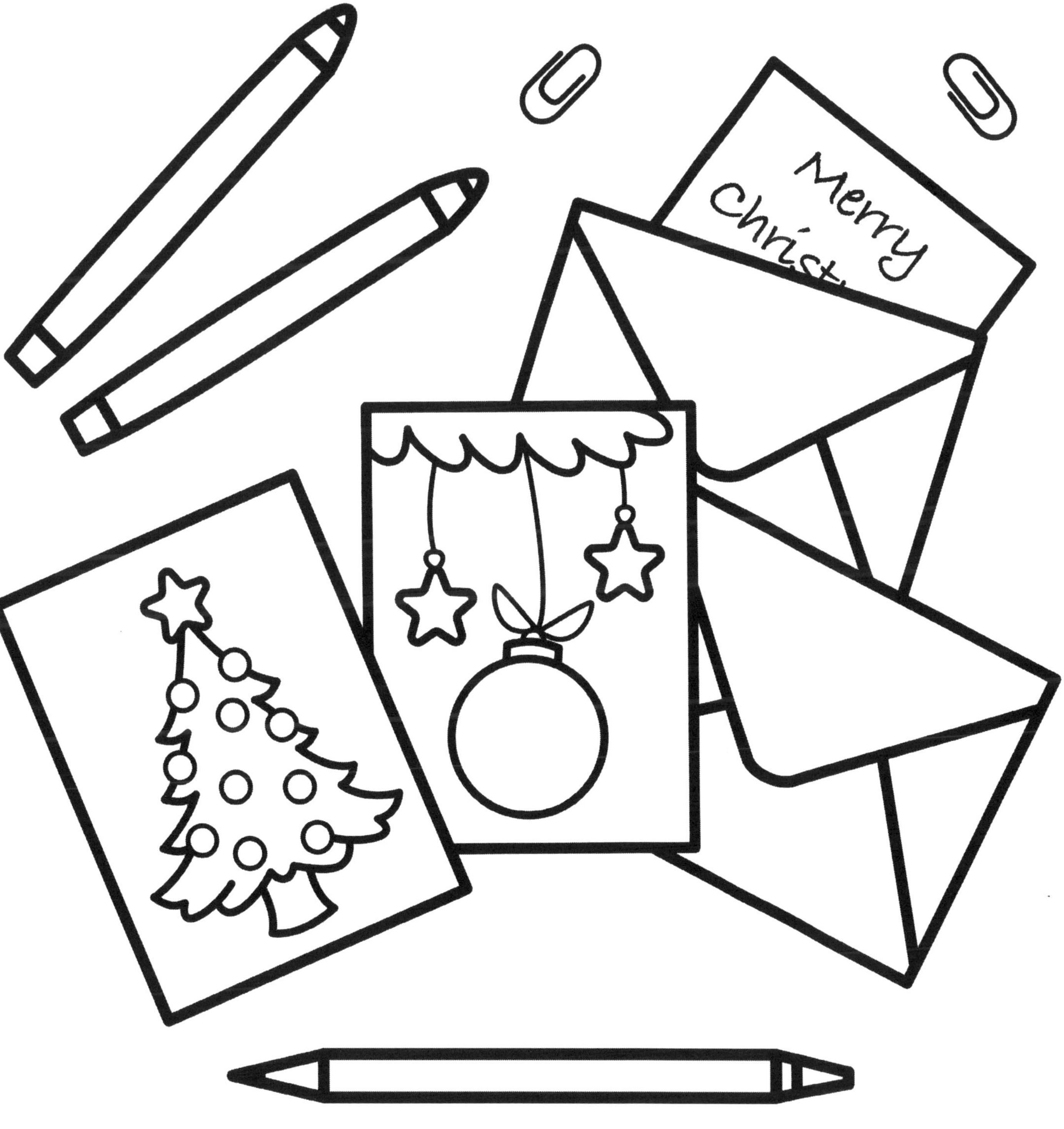
Merry

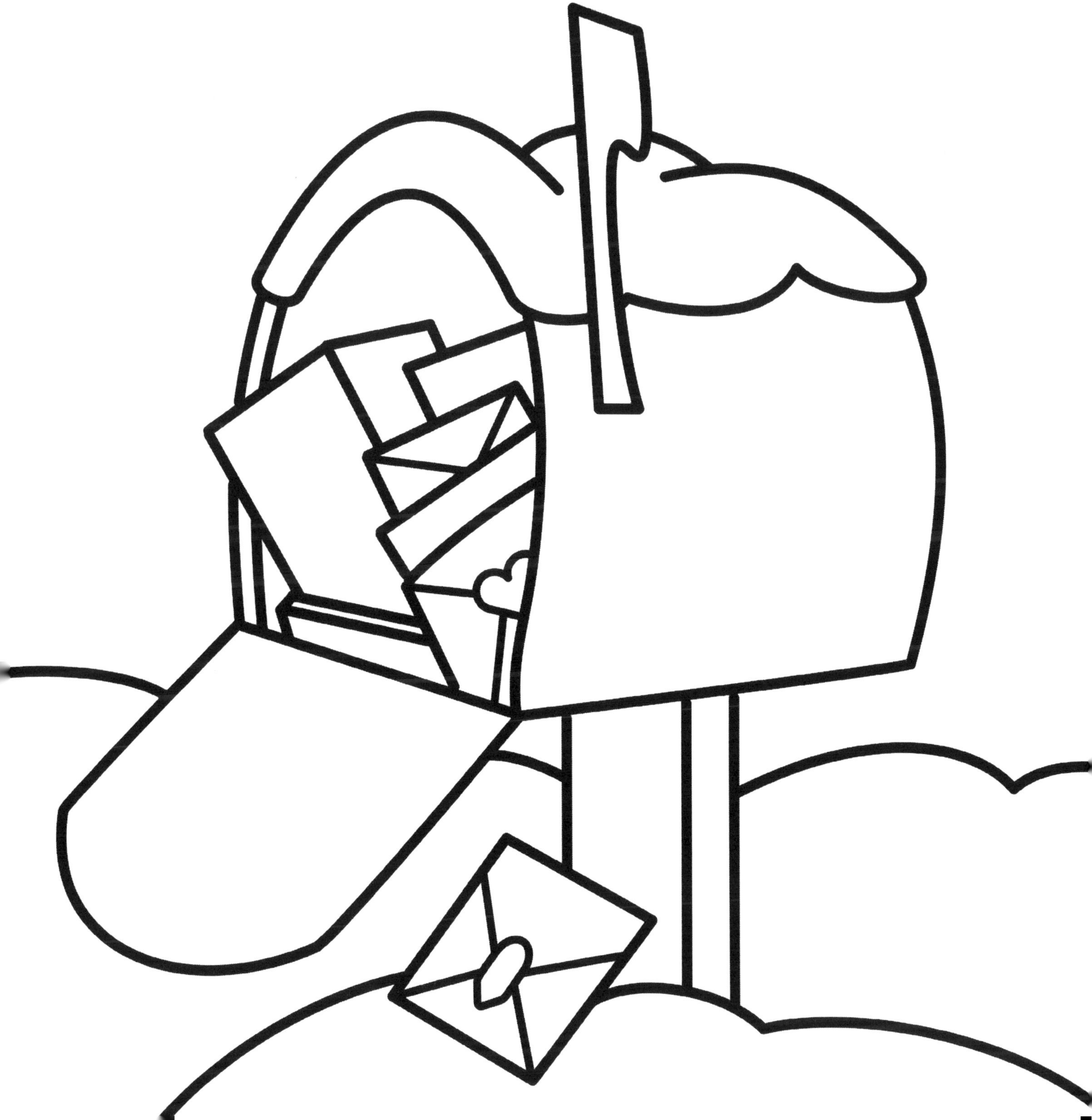

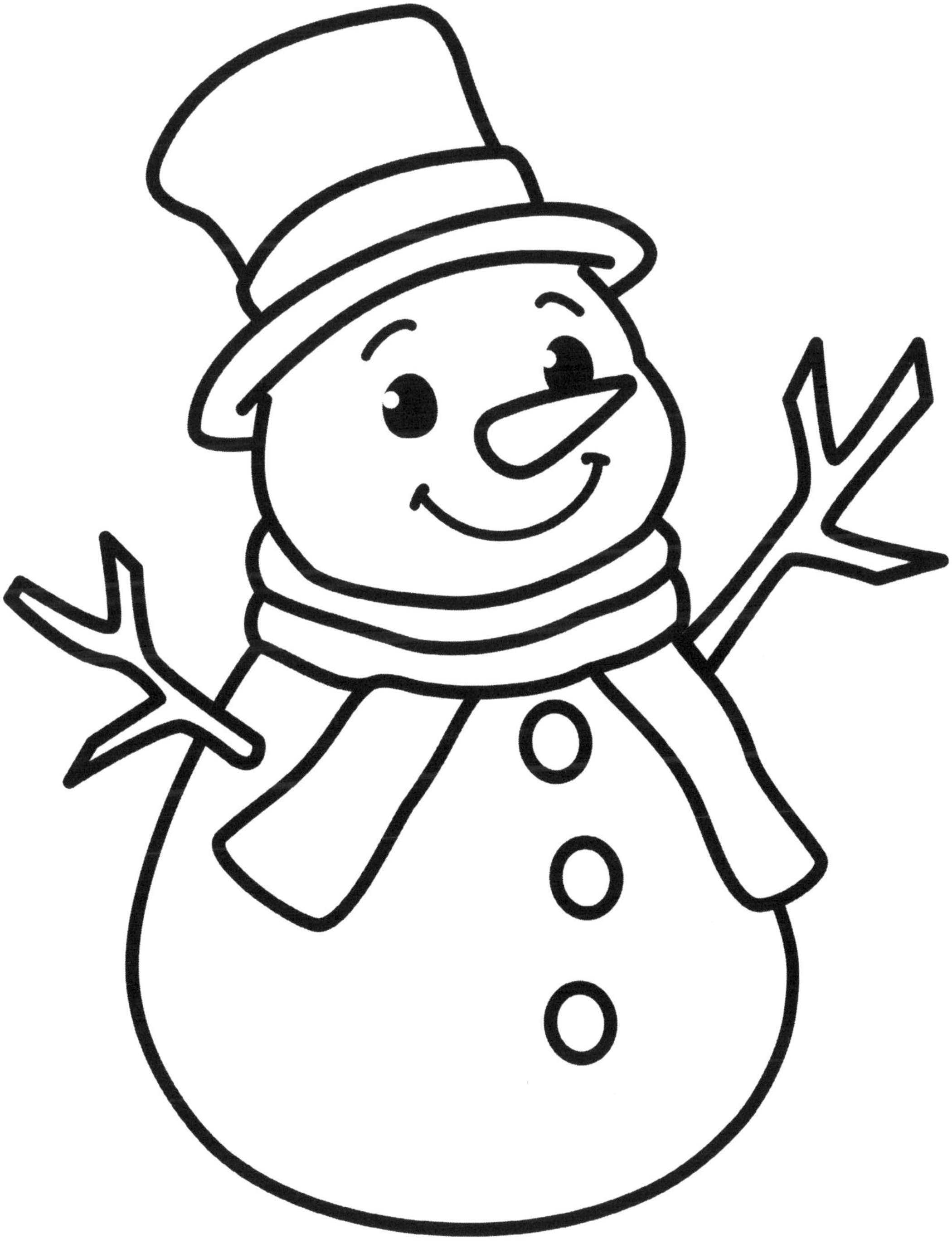

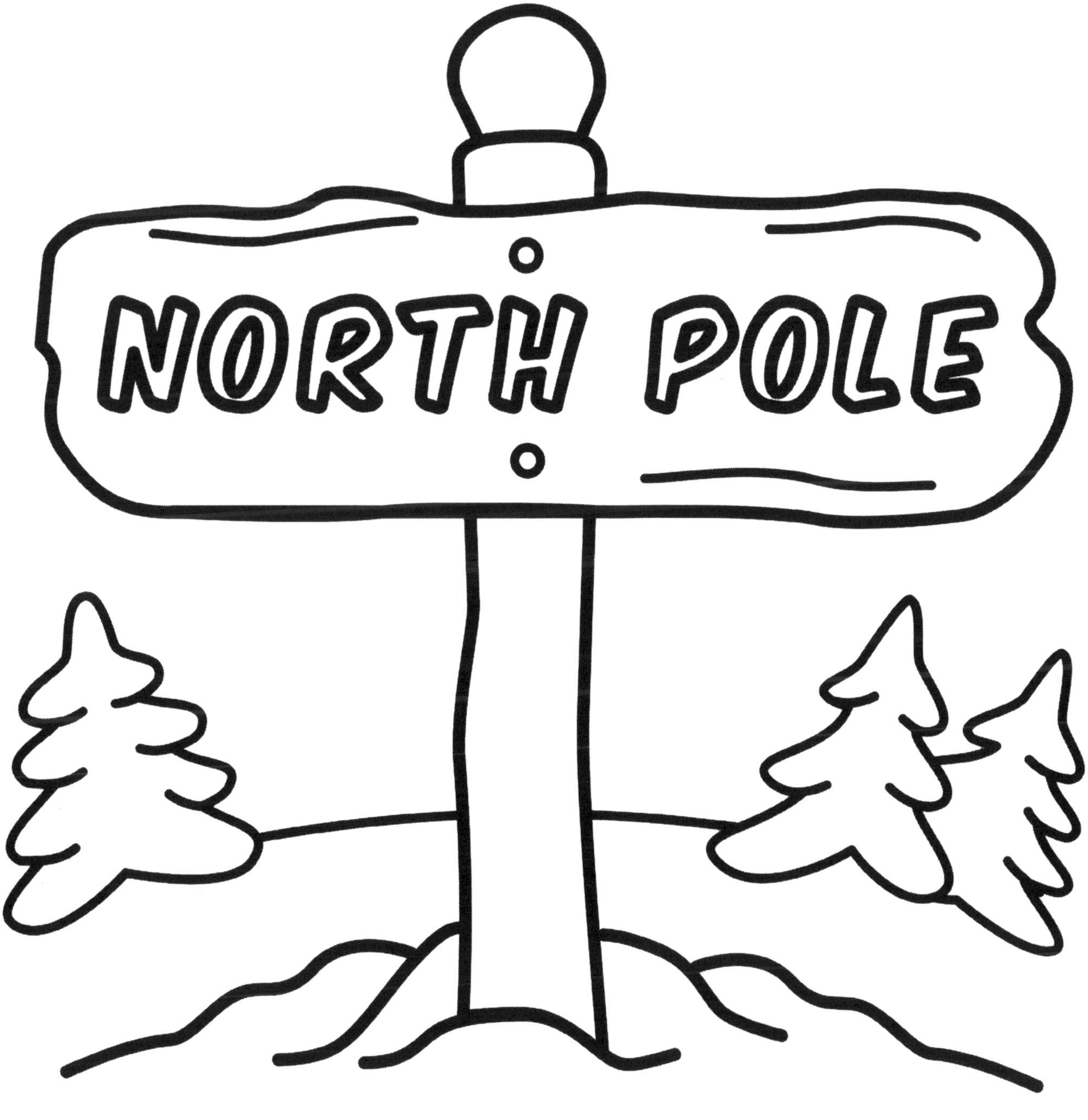
NORTH POLE

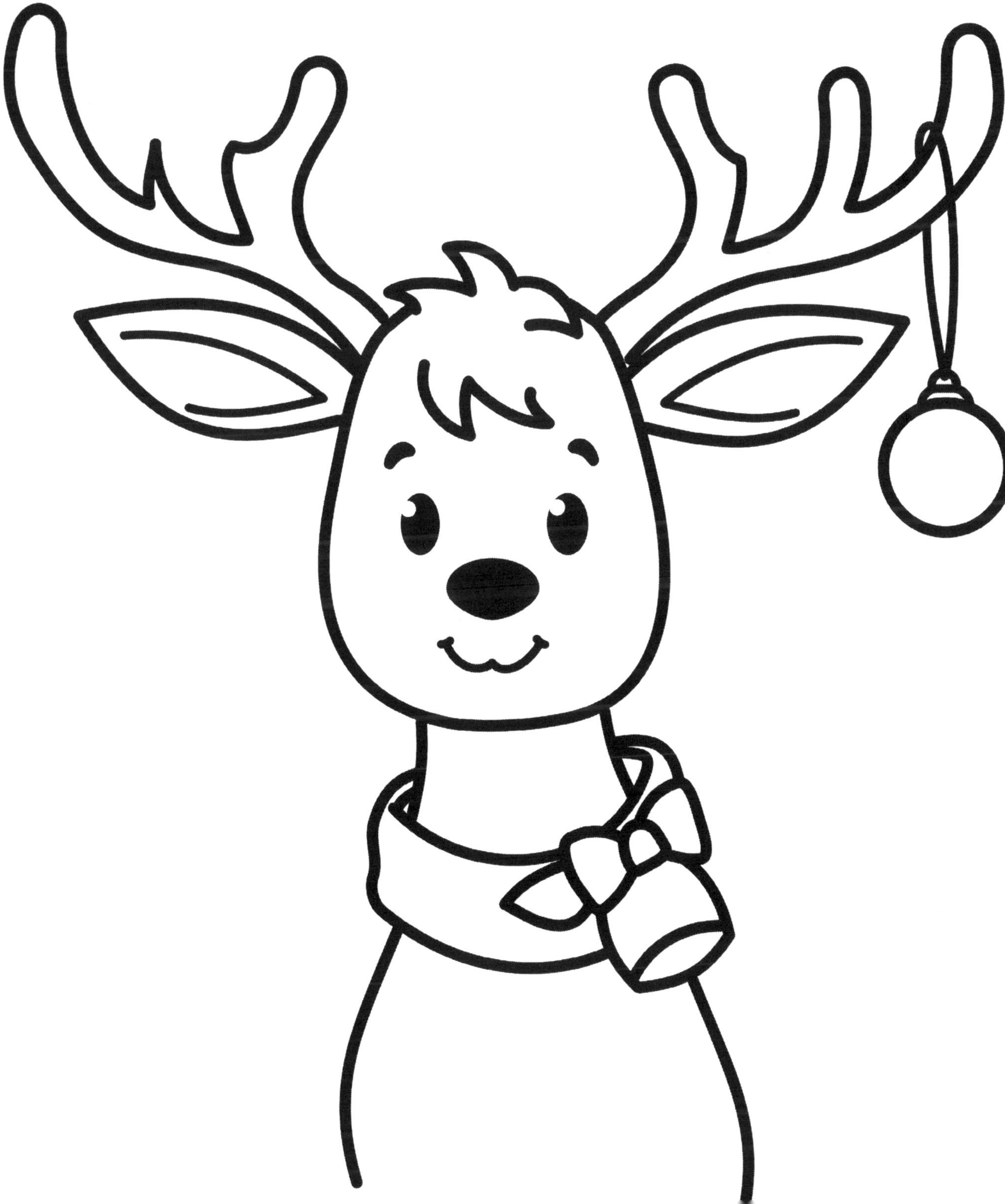

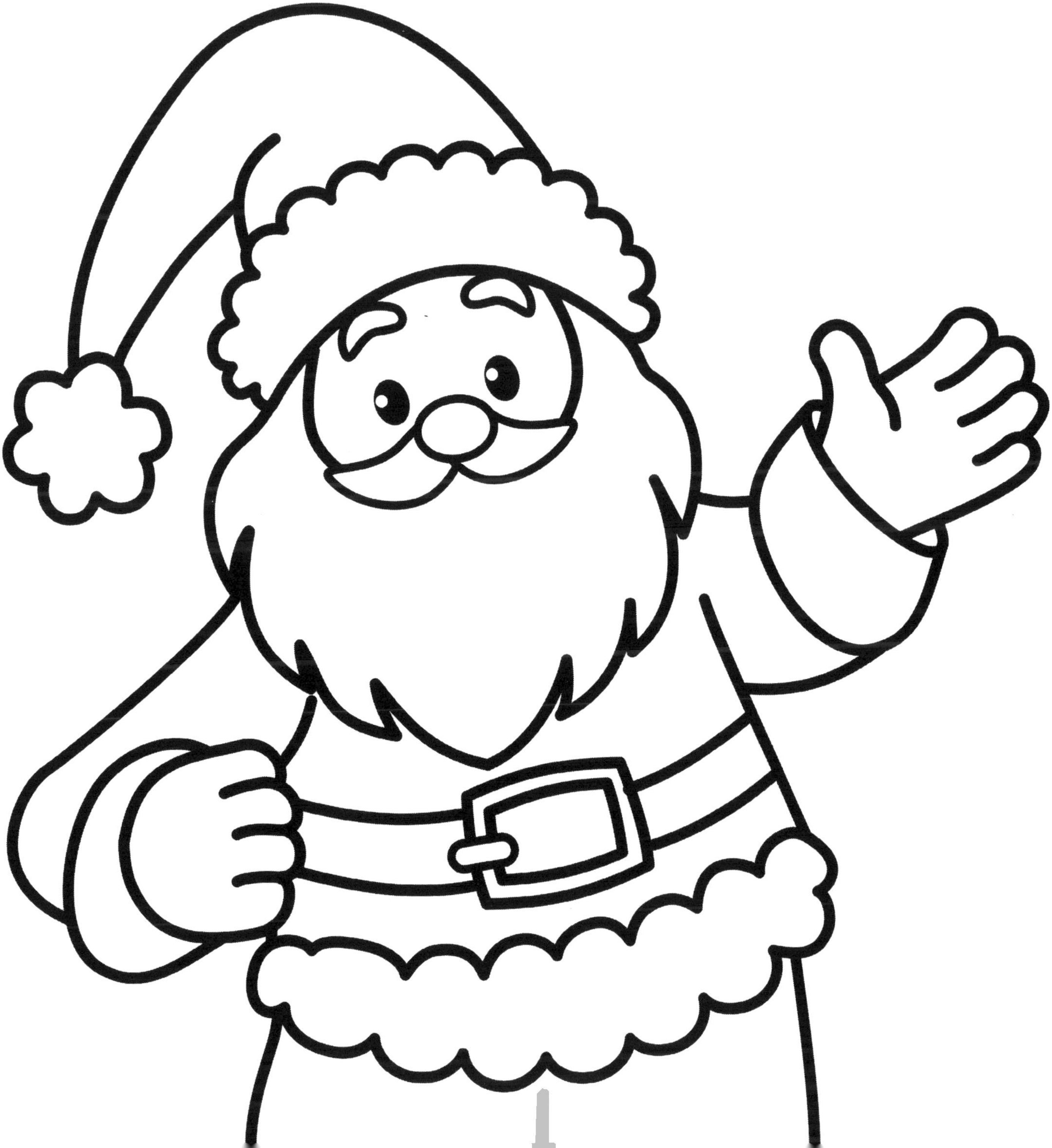

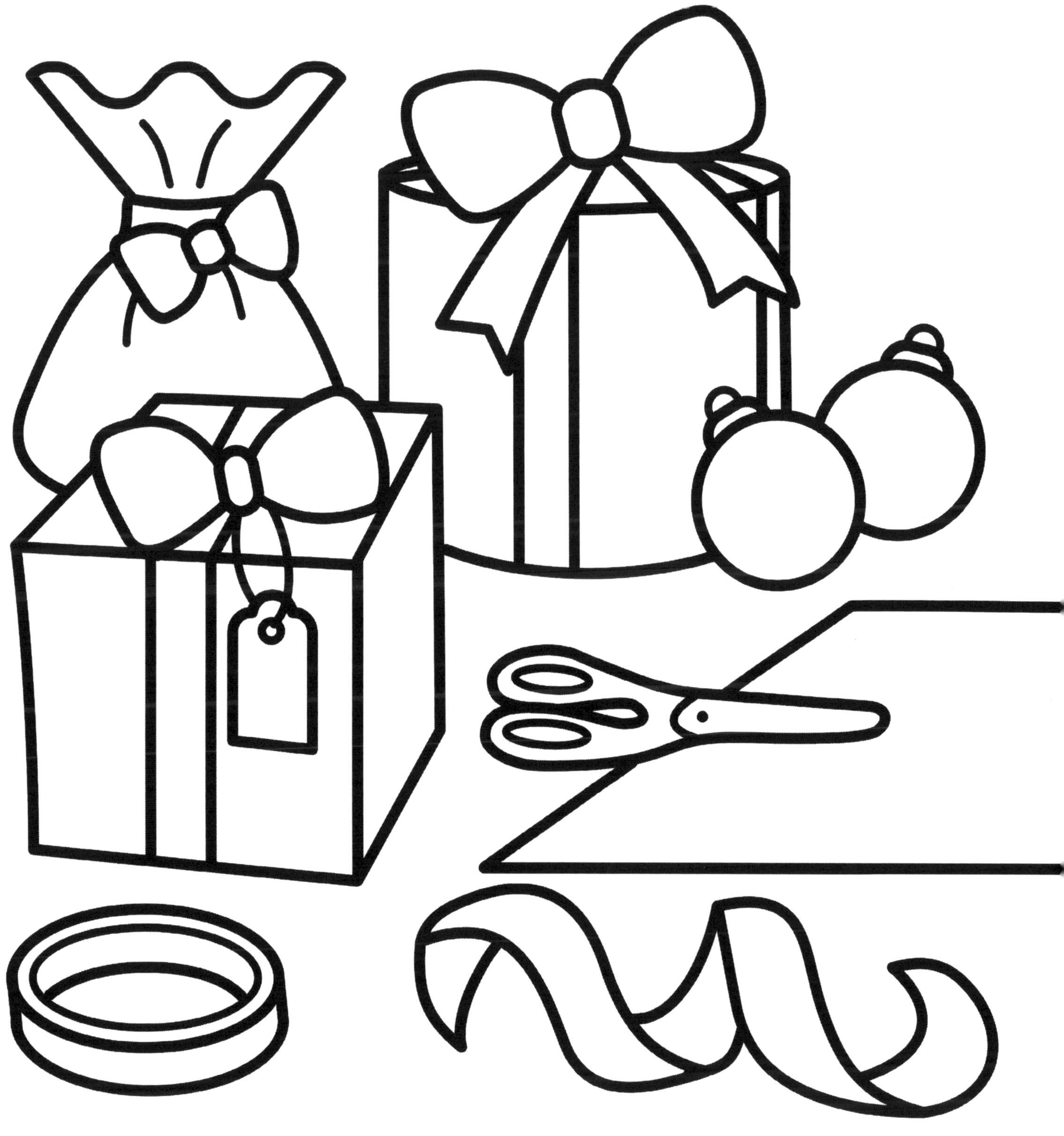

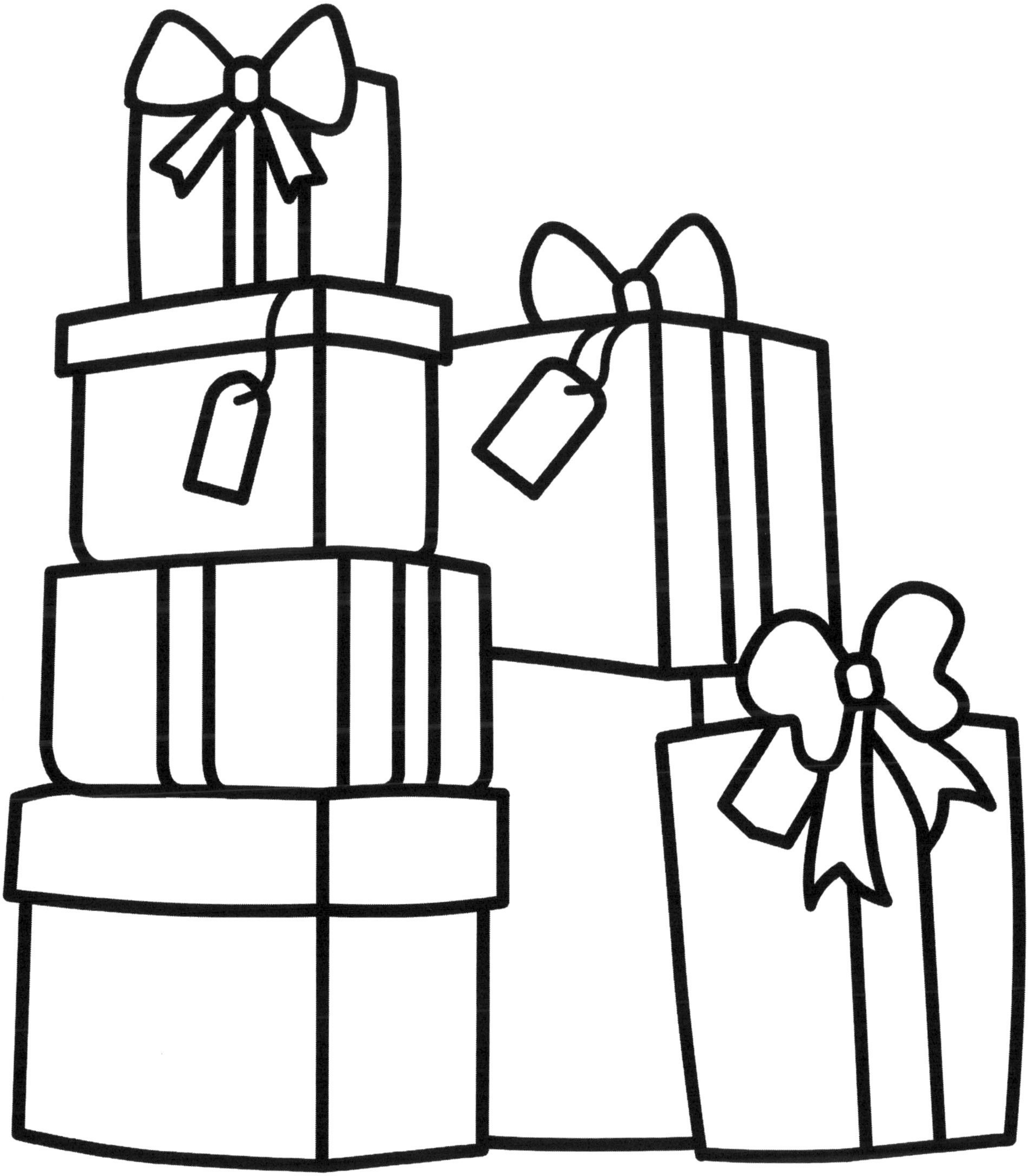

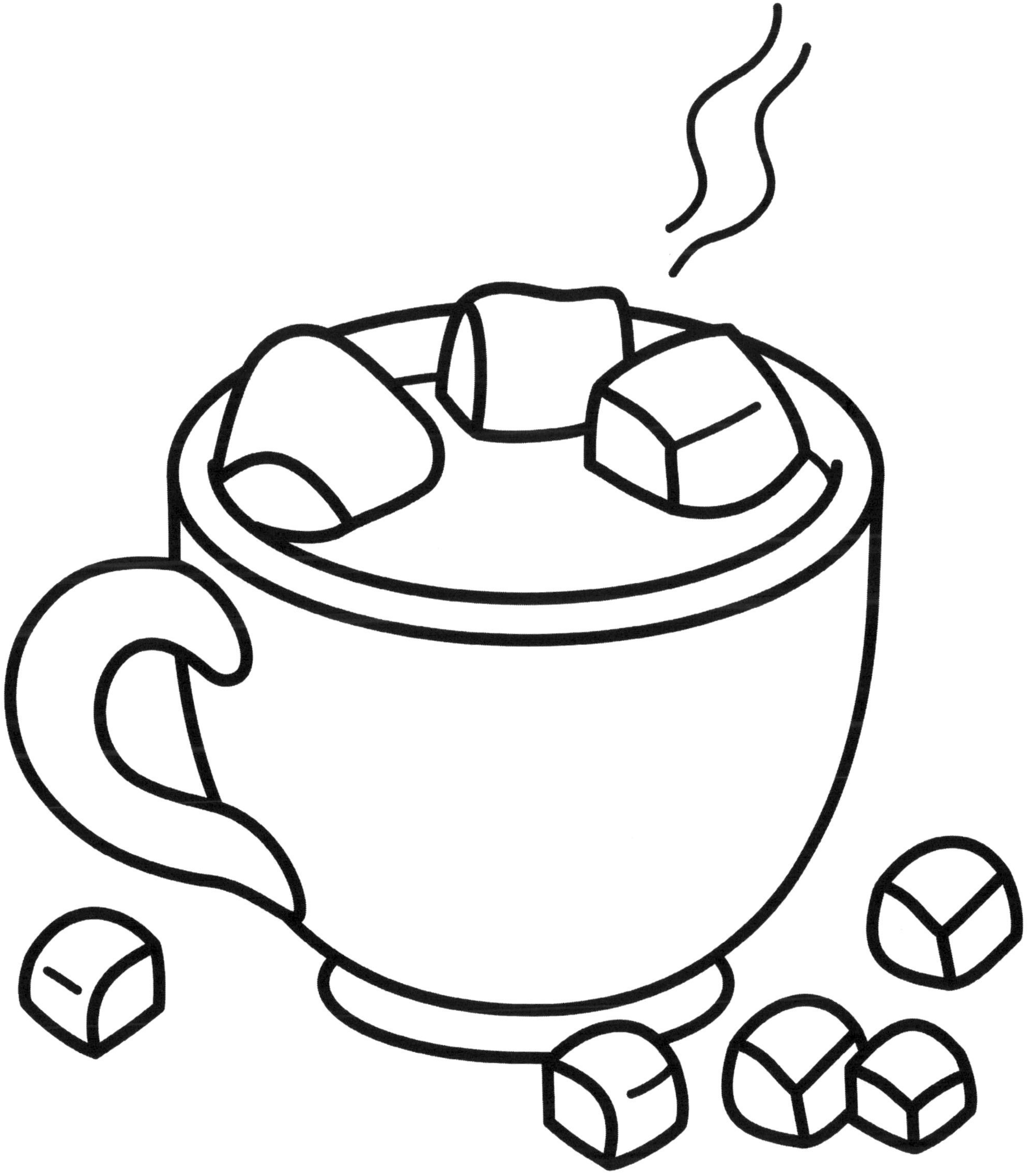

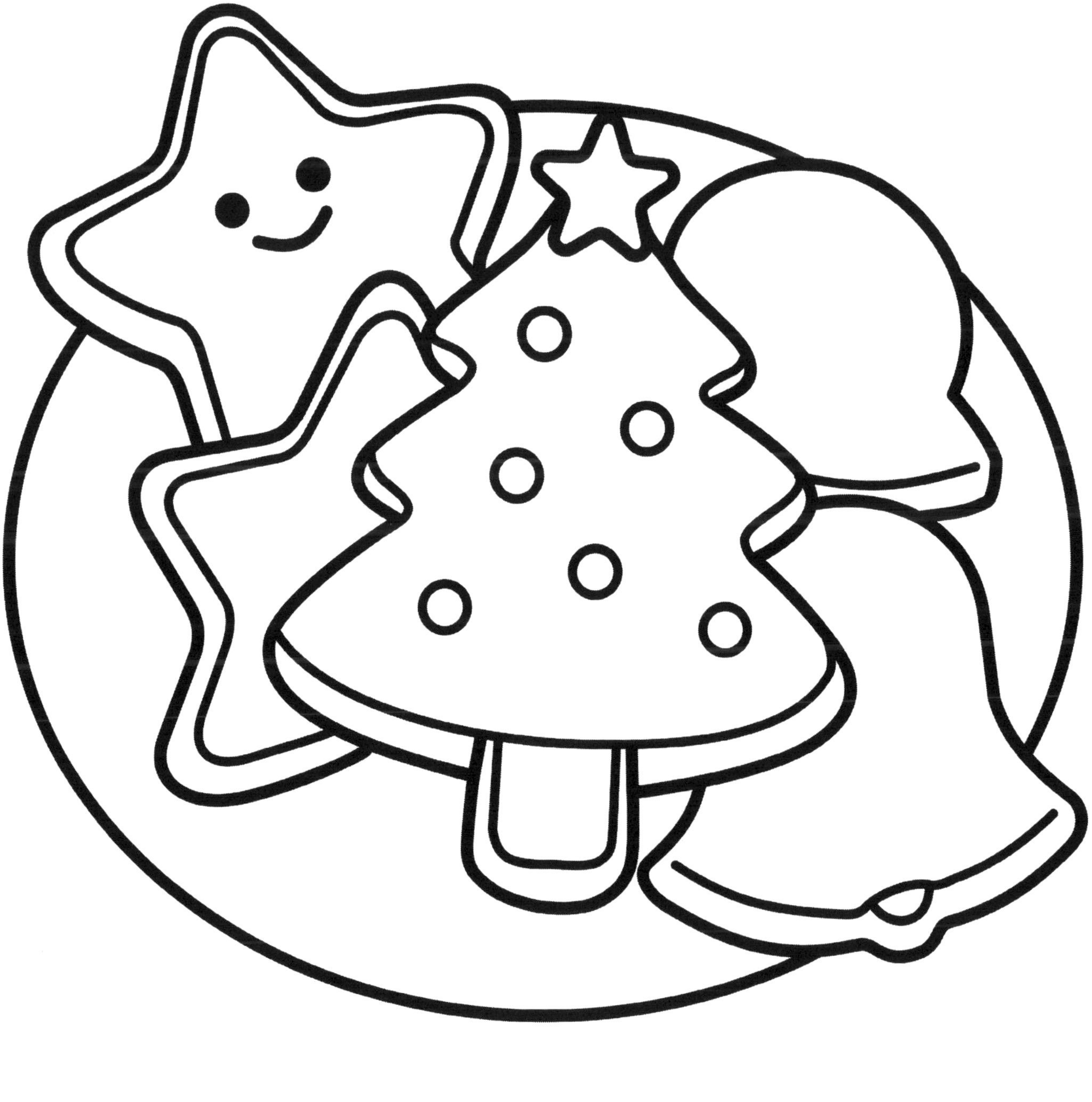

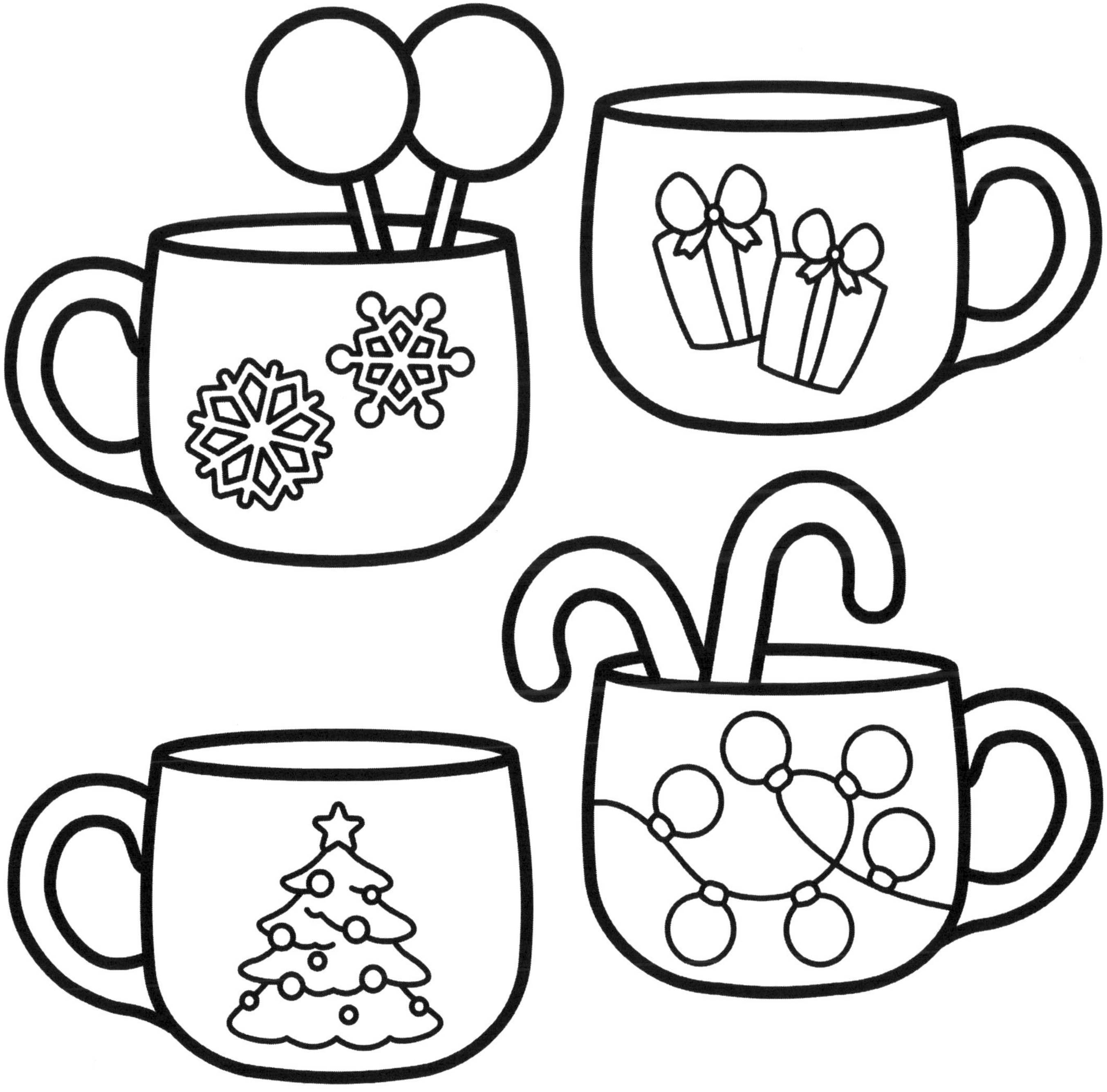

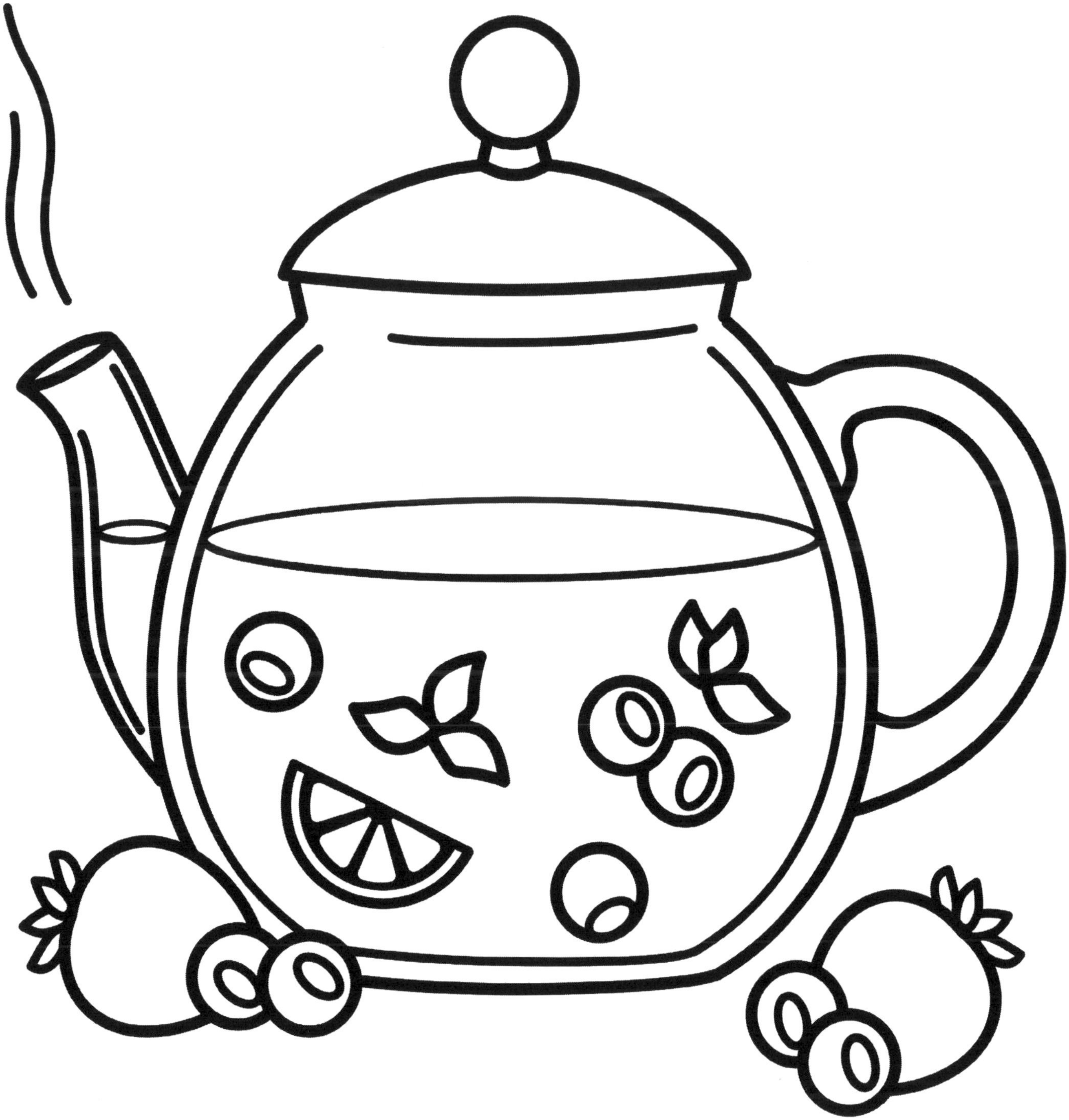

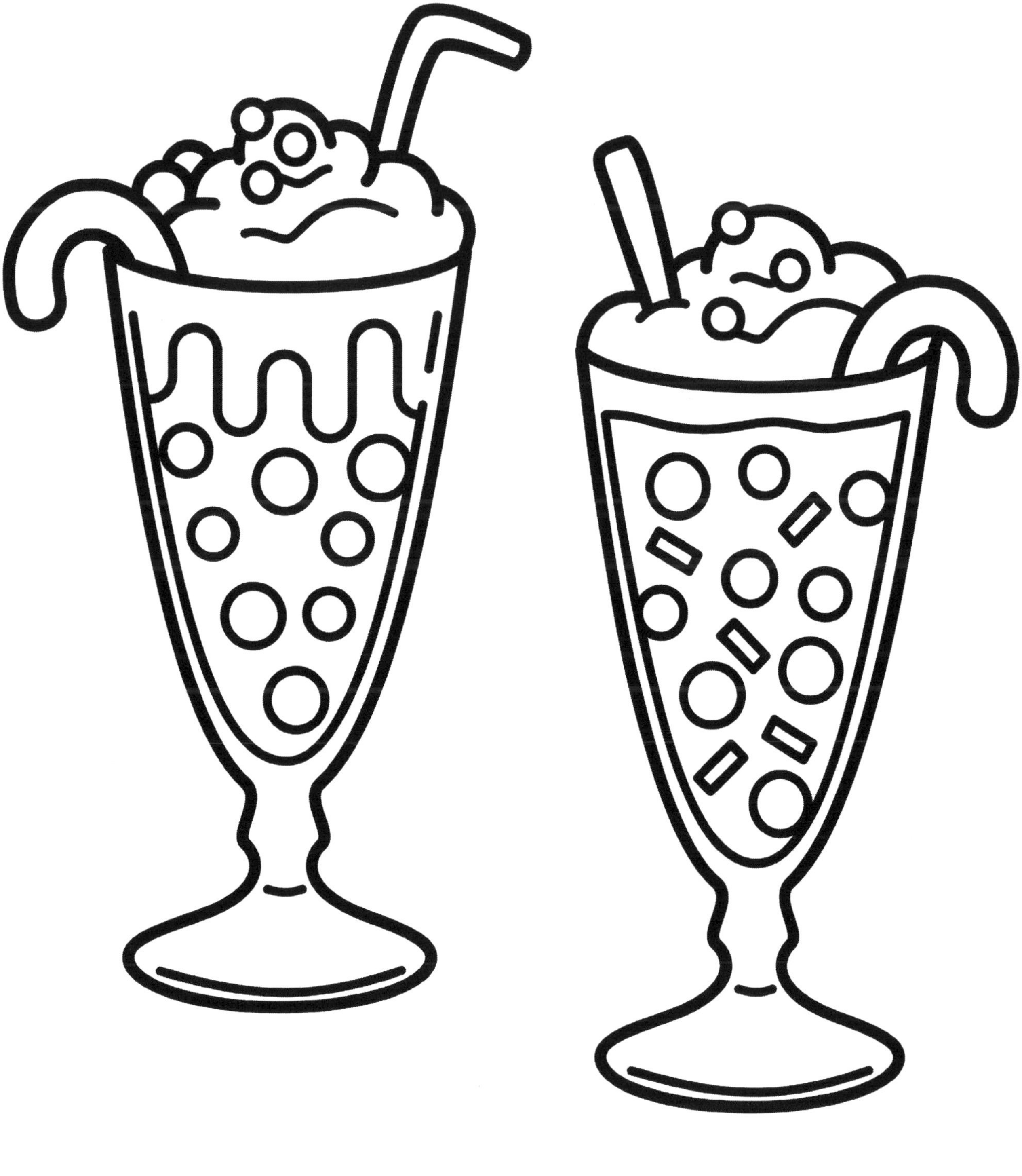

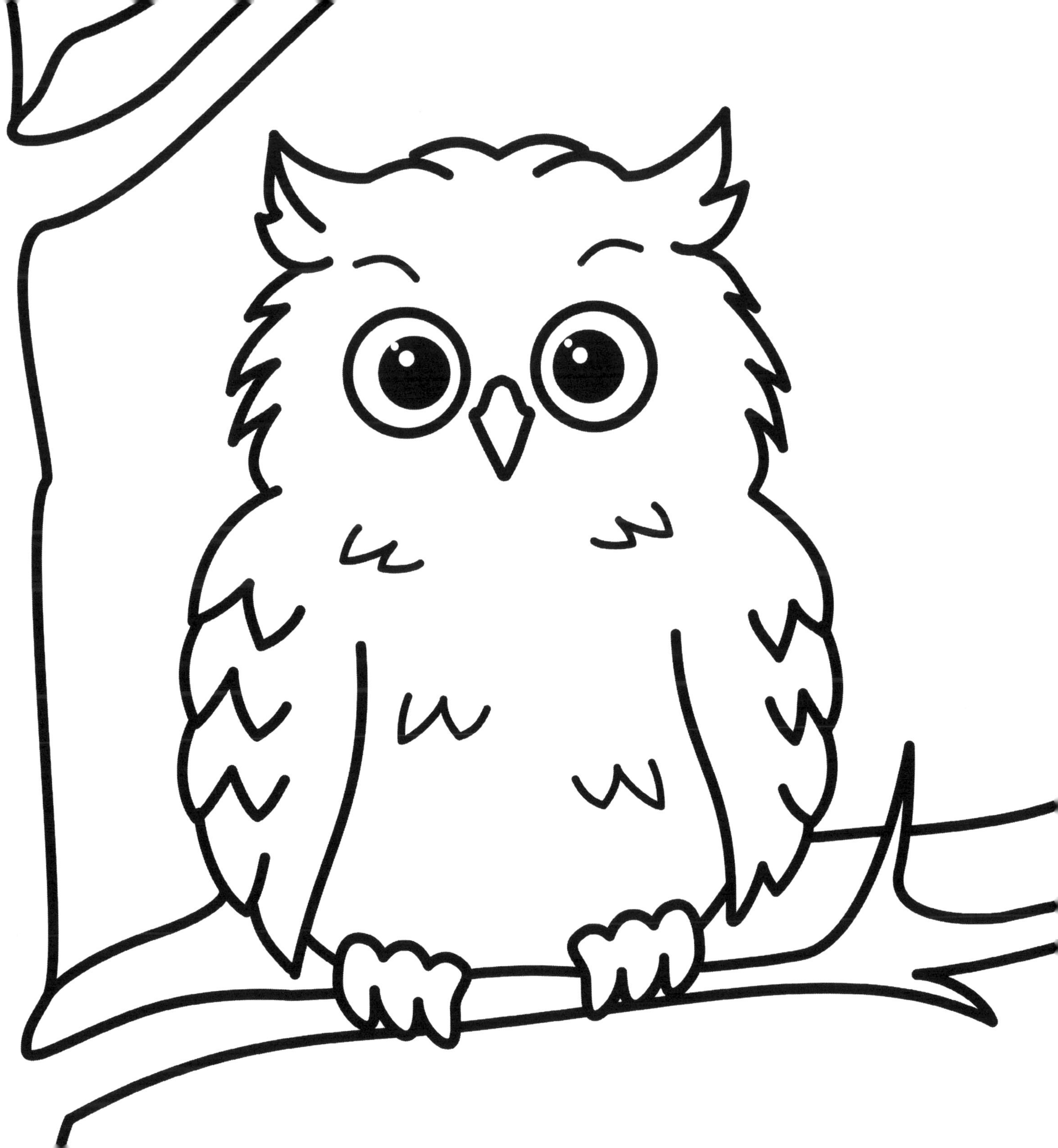

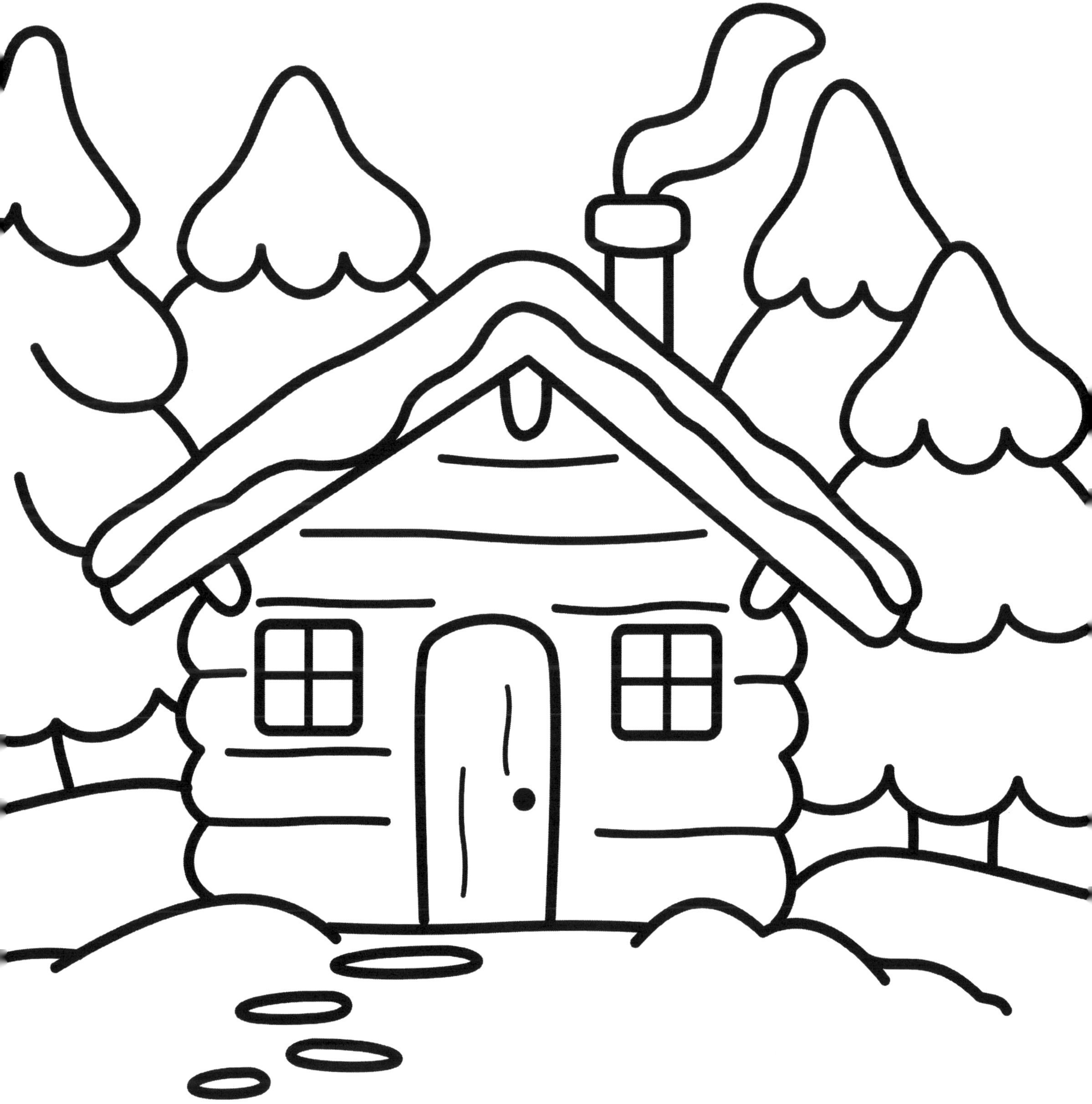

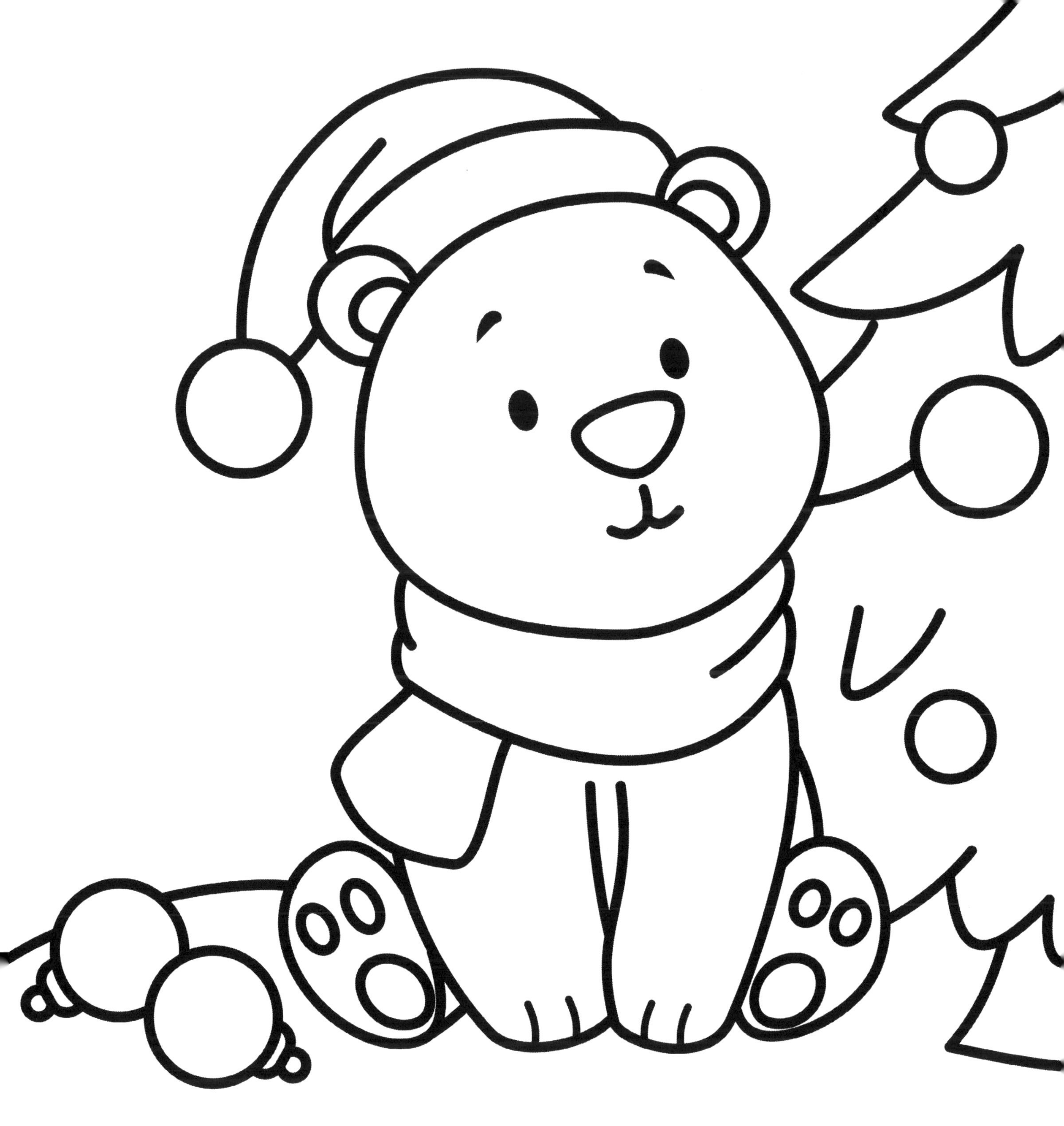

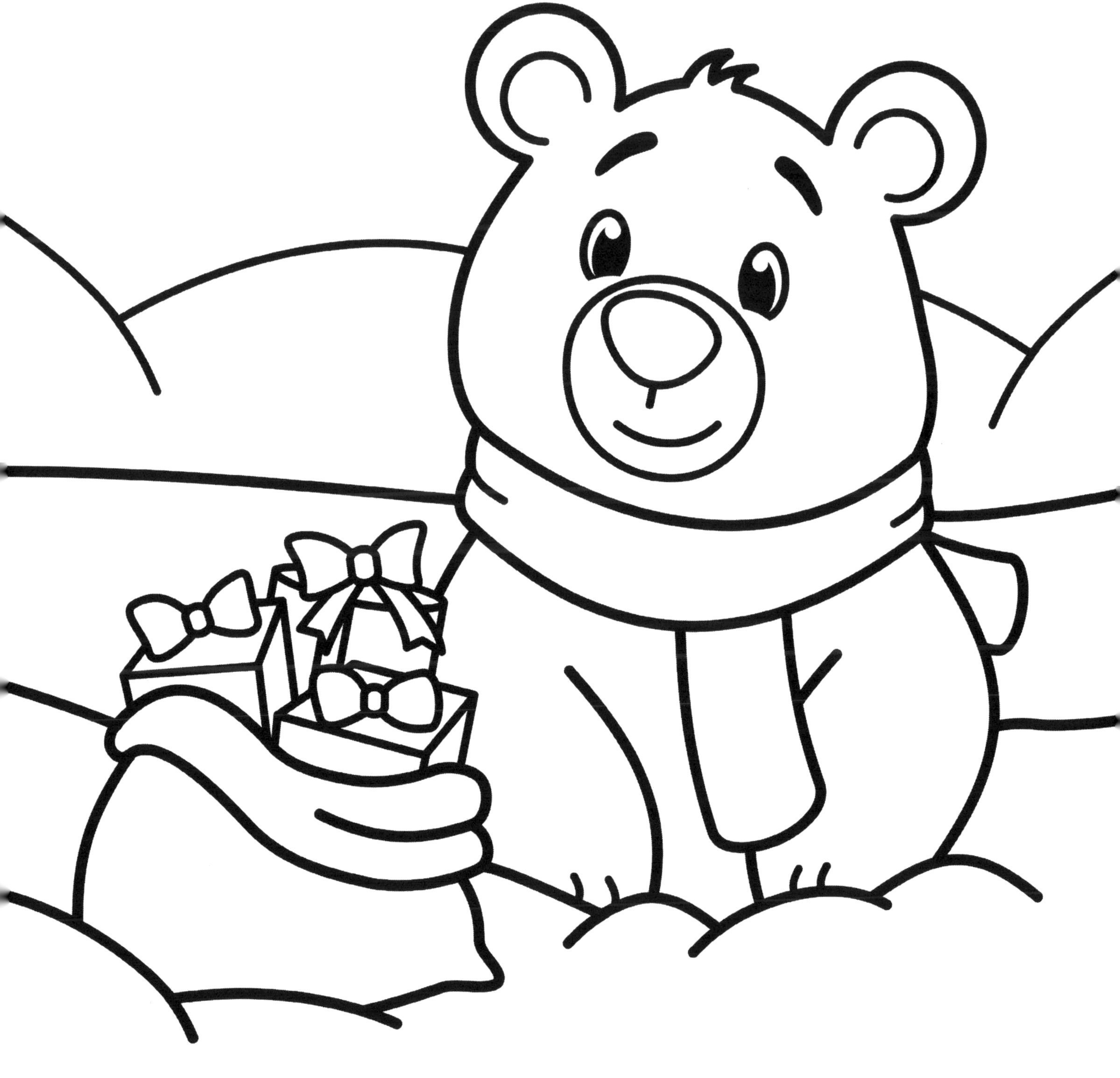

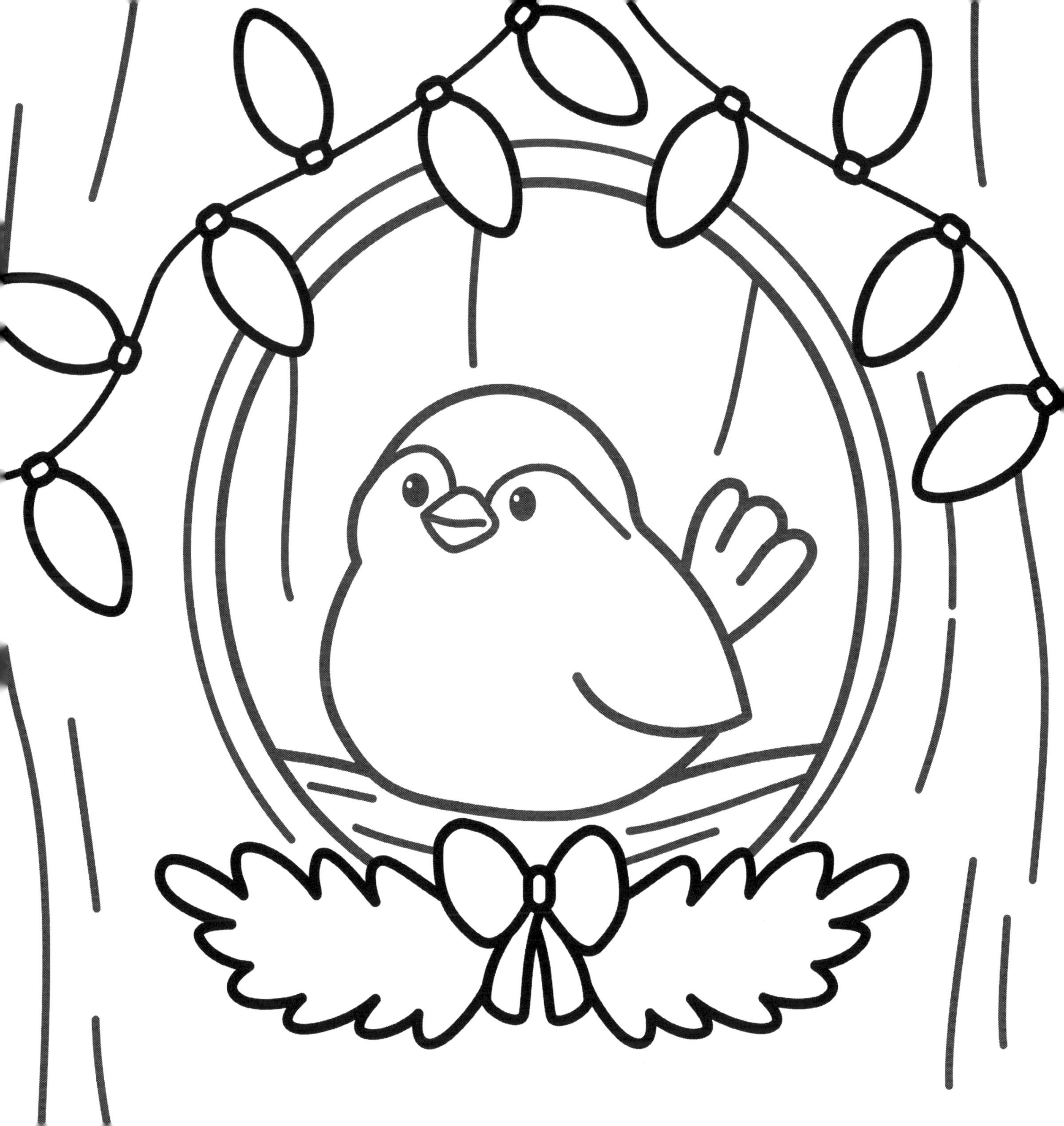

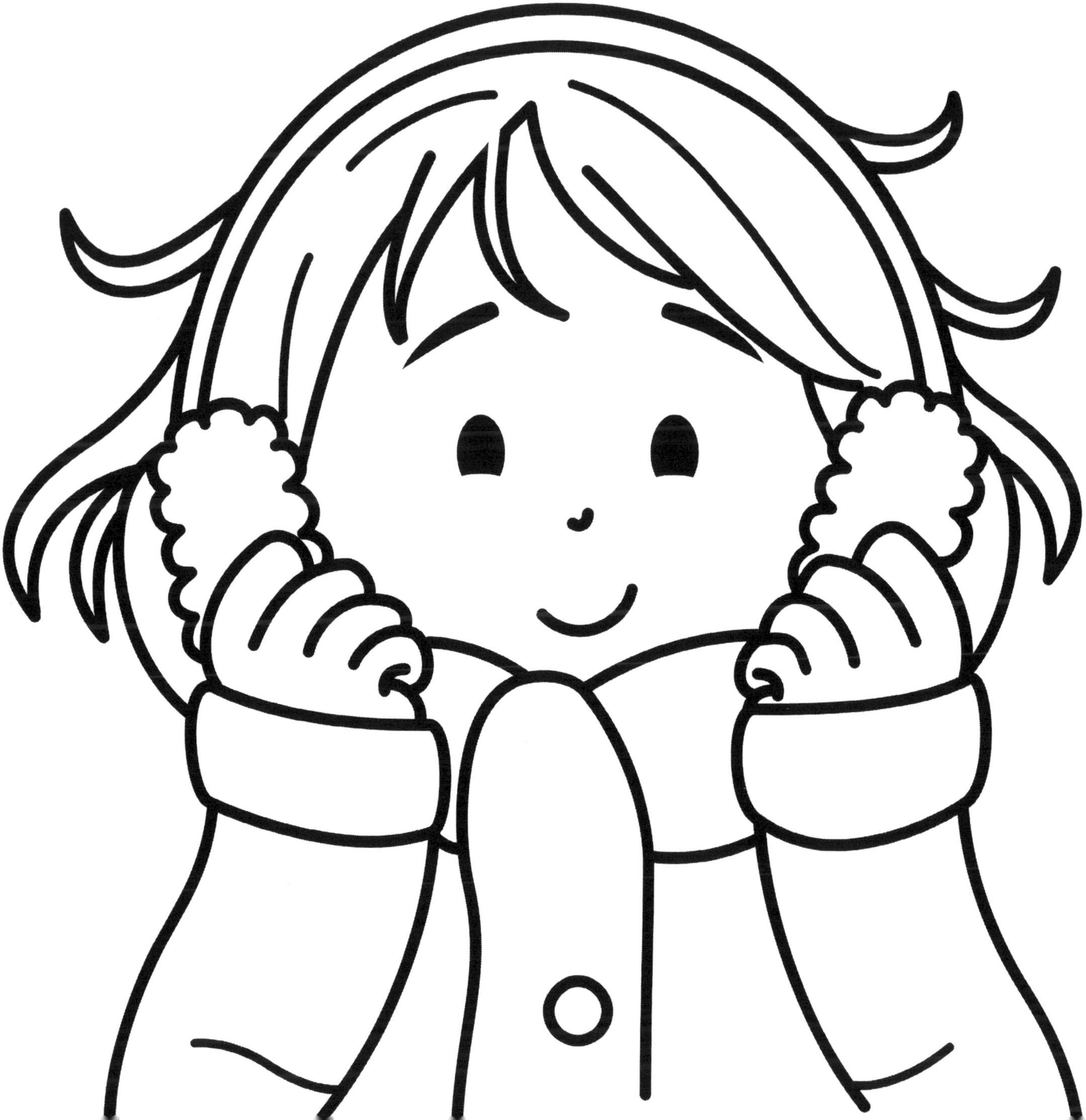

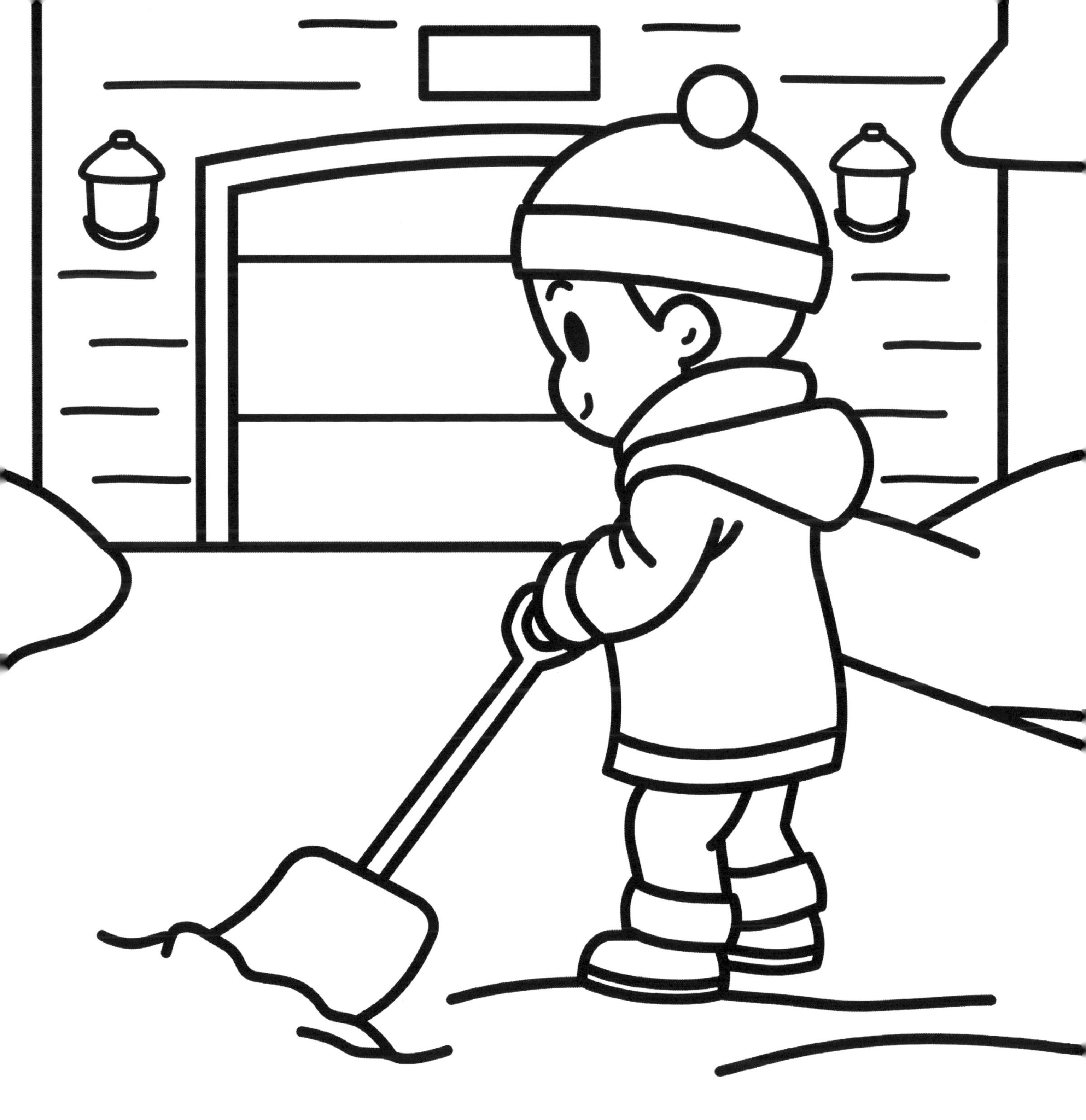

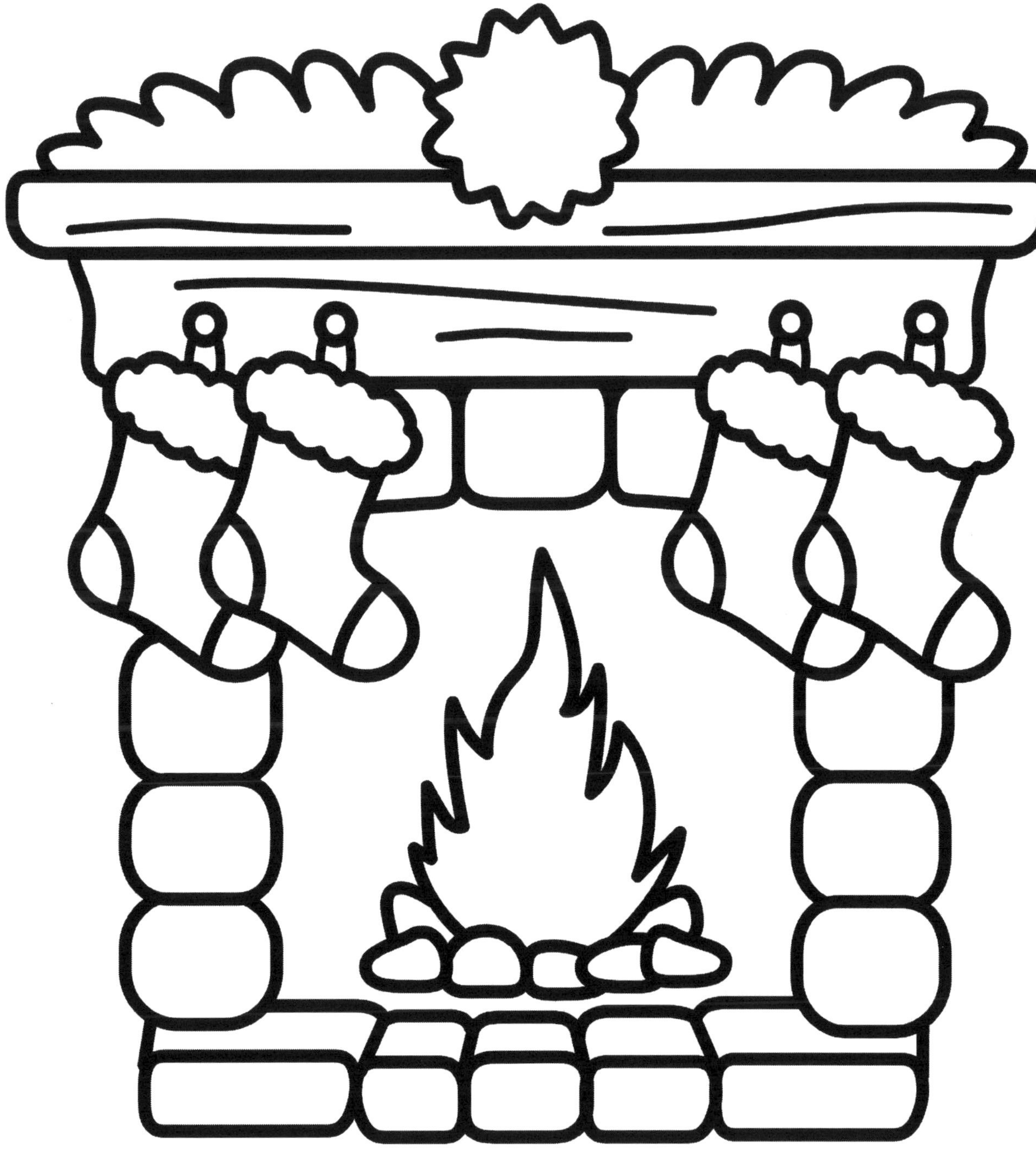

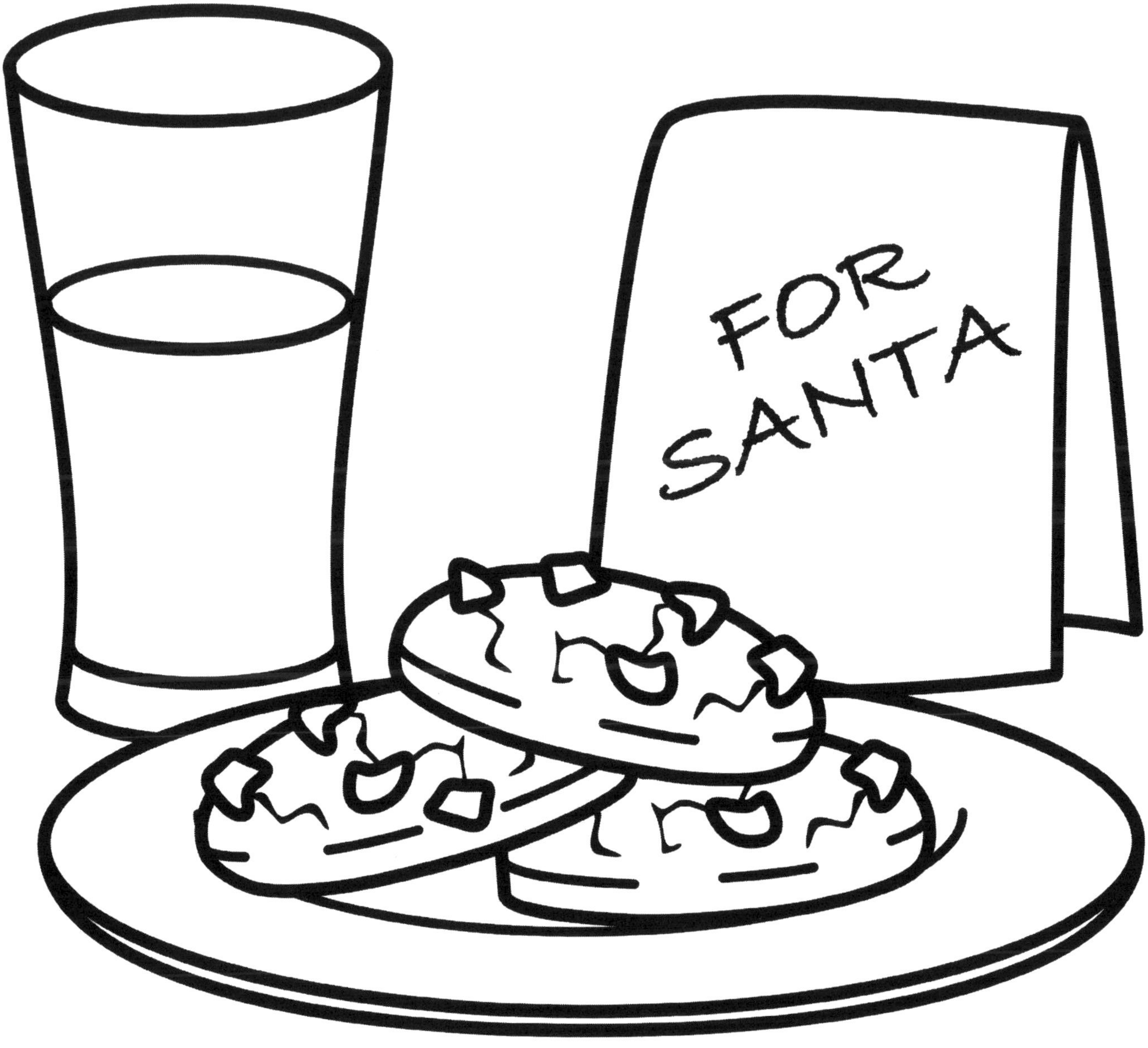
FOR
SANTA

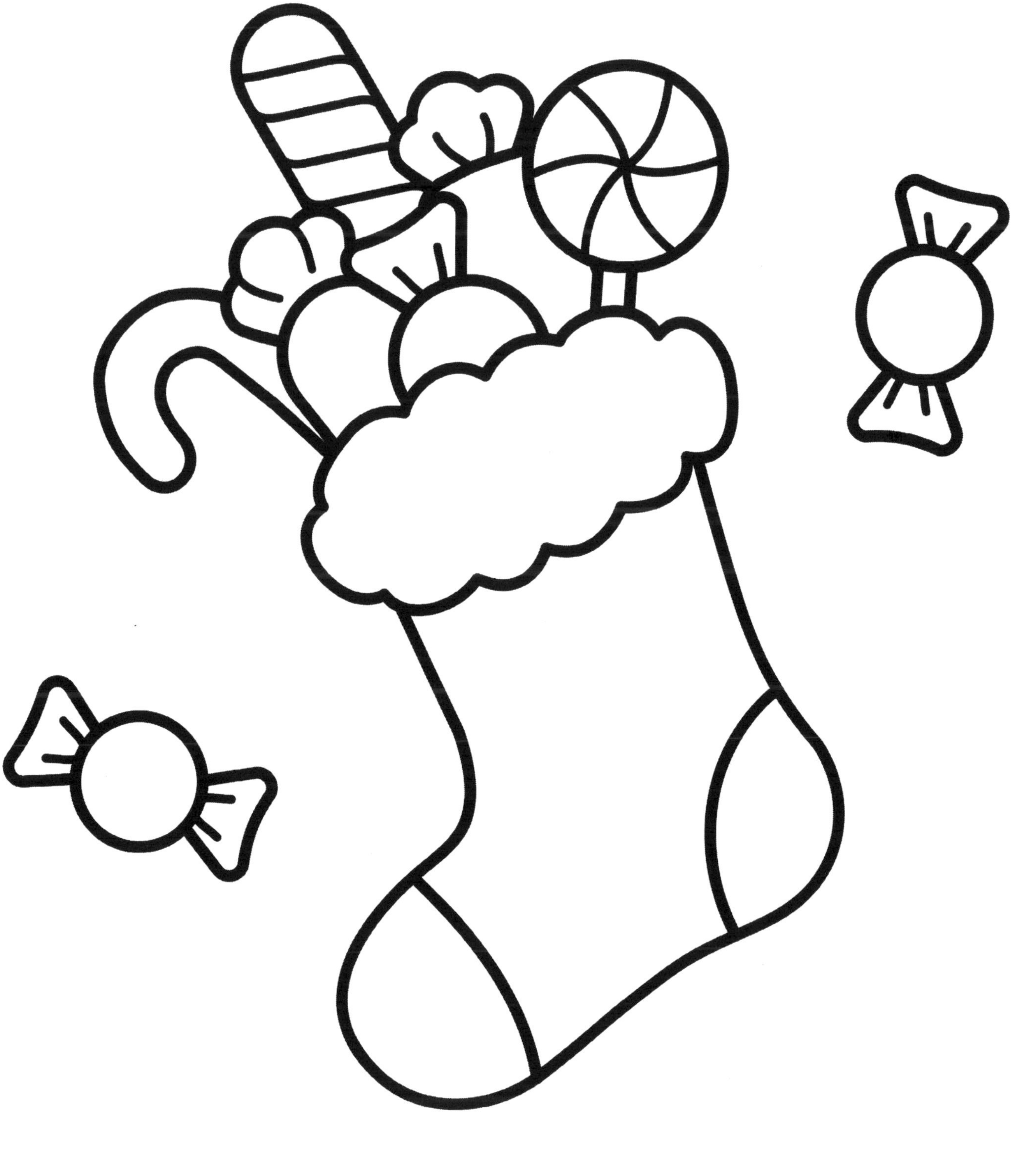

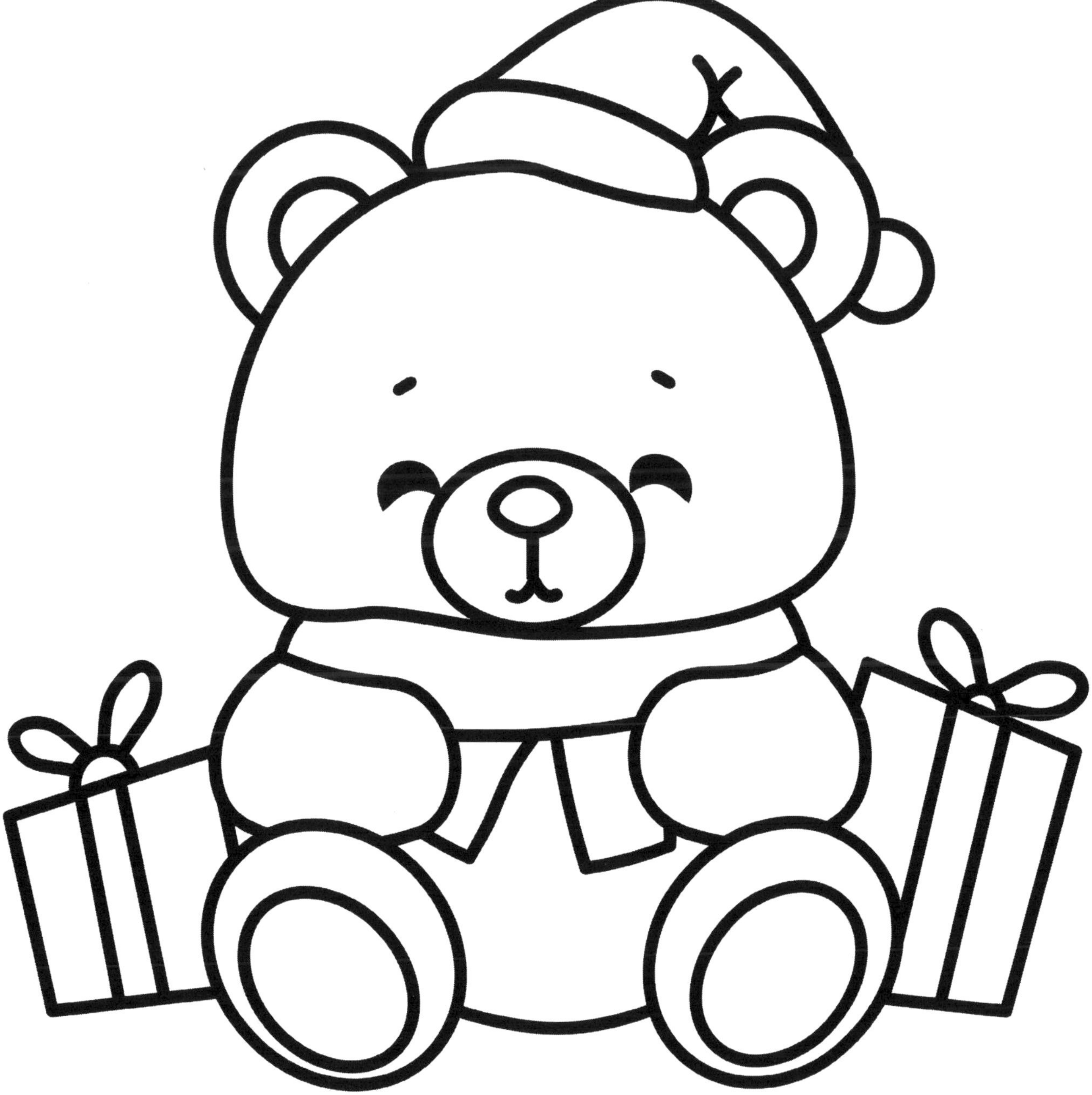

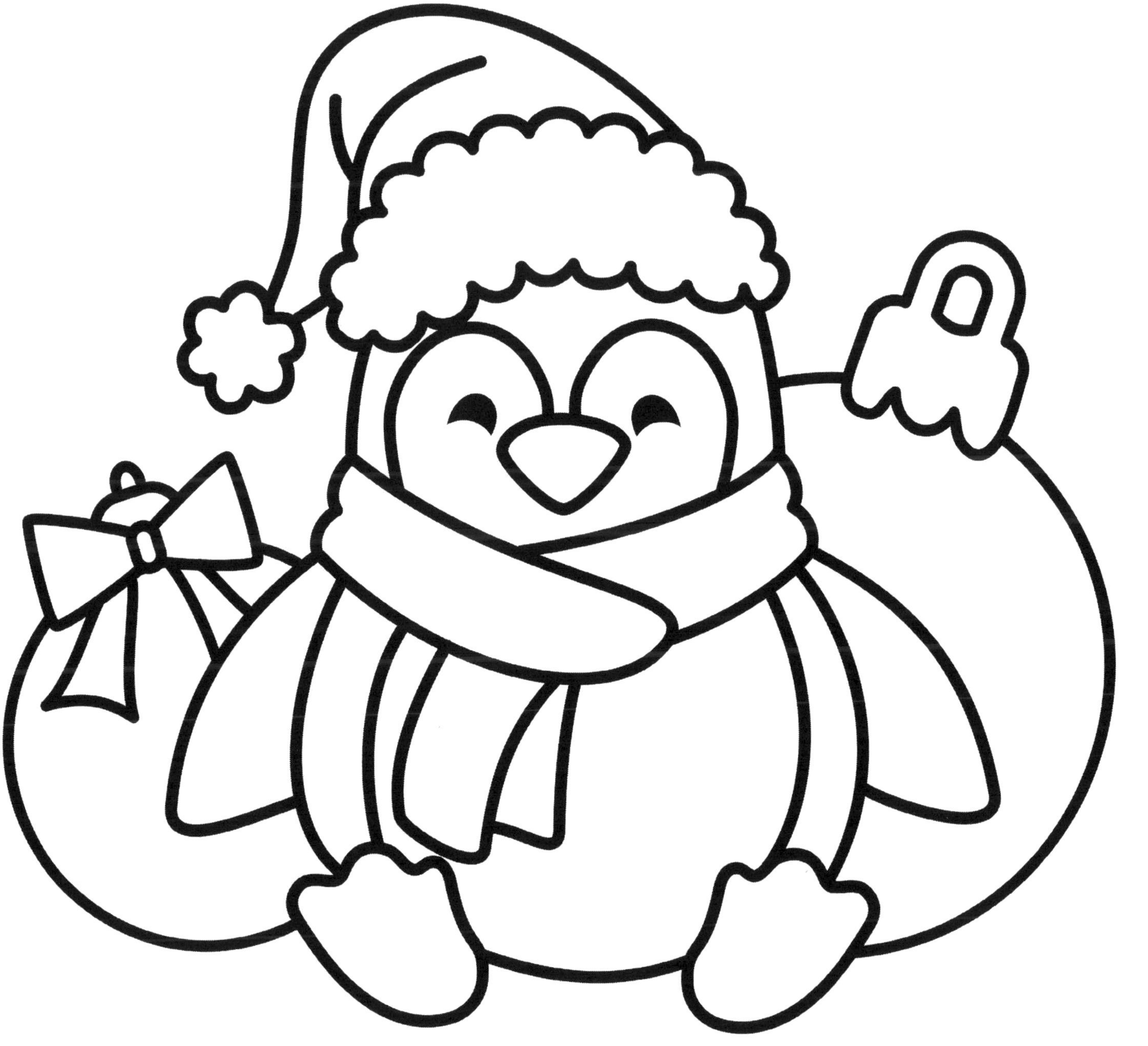

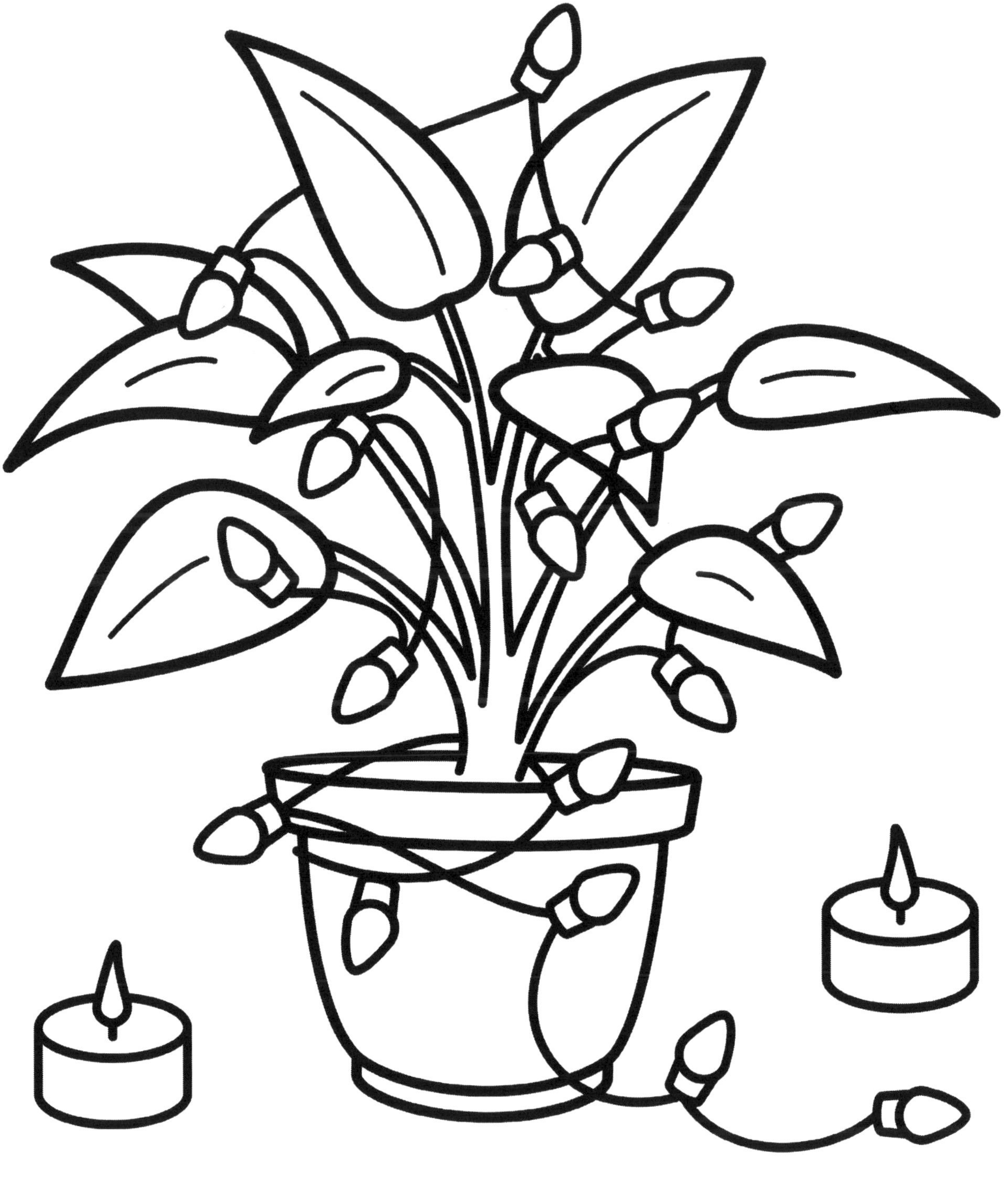

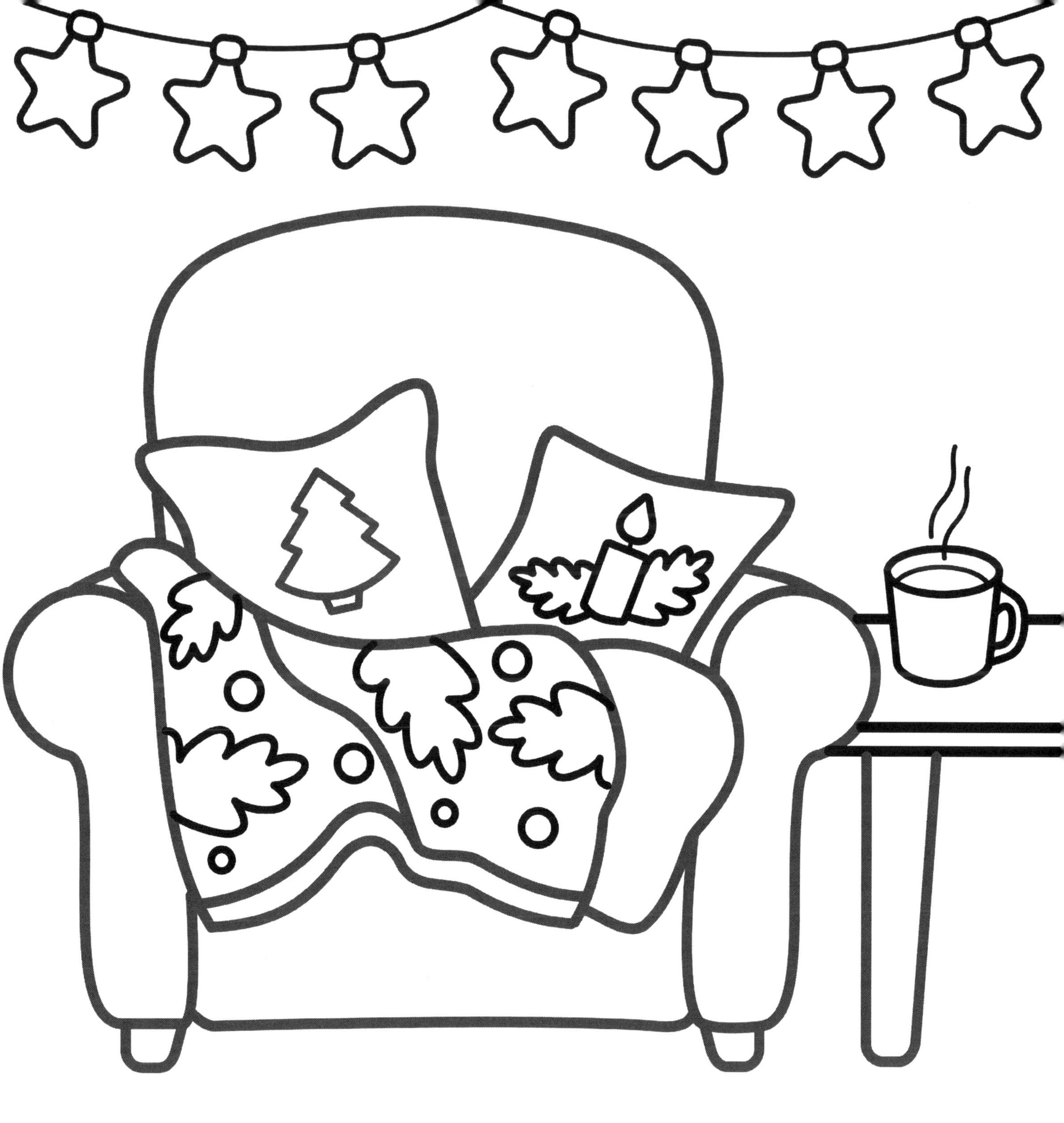

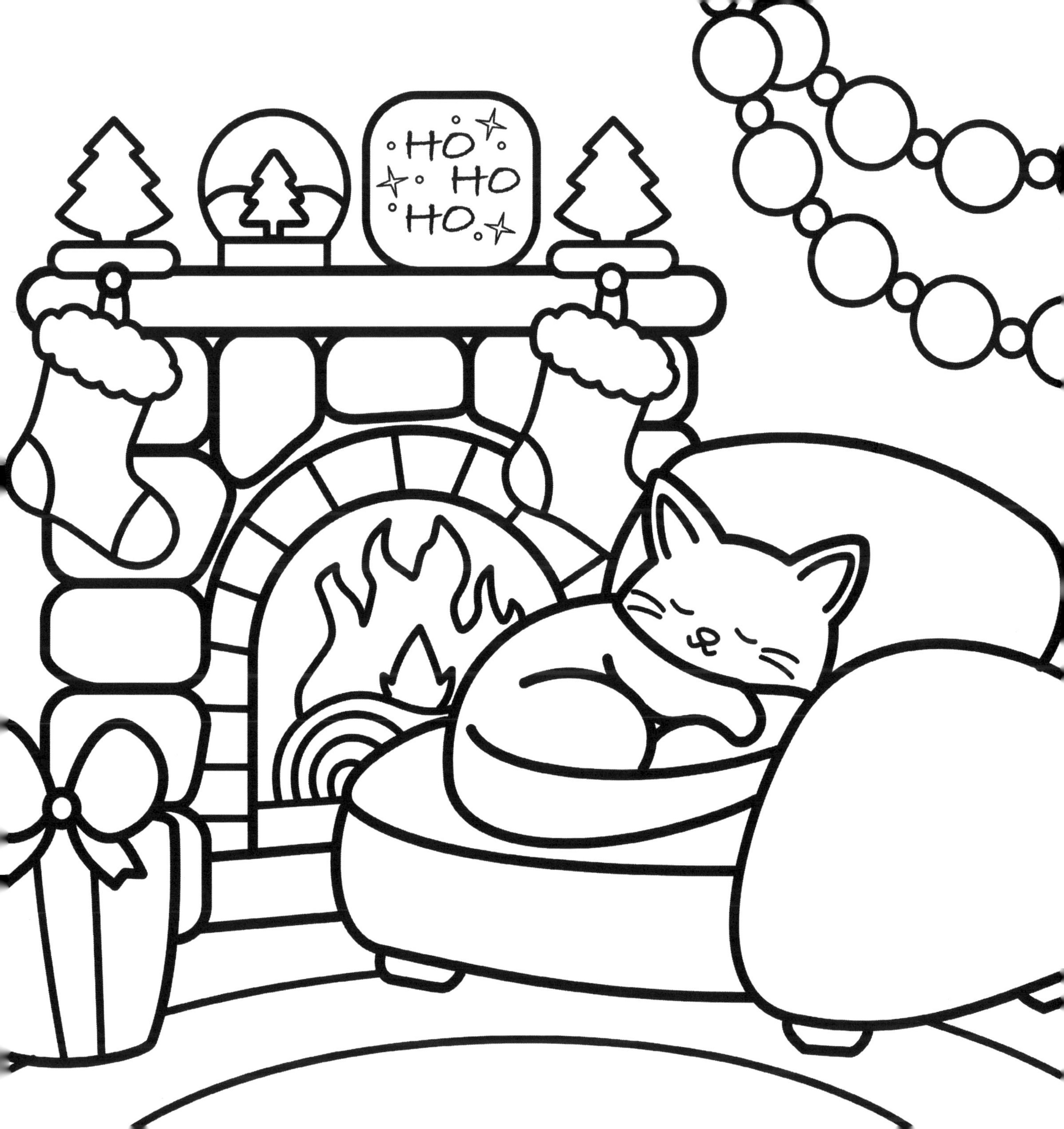
HO
HO HO
HO

Made in the USA
Monee, IL
24 November 2024

71066842R00057